SKILLS IN
HOME ECONOMICS
TEXTILES

Jenny Ridgwell with Louise Davies

HEINEMANN
EDUCATIONAL

Heinemann Educational, a division of
Heinemann Educational Books Ltd
Halley Court, Jordan Hill, Oxford OX2 8EJ

OXFORD LONDON EDINBURGH
MELBOURNE SYDNEY AUCKLAND
IBADAN NAIROBI GABORONE HARARE
KINGSTON PORTSMOUTH NH (USA)
SINGAPORE MADRID

© Jenny Ridgwell and Louise Davies 1989

First published 1989

British Library Cataloguing in Publication Data
Ridgwell, Jenny
Skills in home economics: textiles
1. Textiles – for schools
I. Title II. Davies, Louise
677
ISBN 0 435 42001 1

Designed and produced by
The Pen and Ink Book Co. Ltd., Huntingdon, Cambridgeshire

Printed and bound in Spain by Mateu Cromo

Acknowledgements

Thanks are due to the following for permission to reproduce copyright material: British Home Stores plc for the care labels on pp. 22, 25 and 85; British Wool Marketing Board for the label on p. 89; Christian Aid for the material on recycling on p. 31; *Daily Mail* for the adapted article on p. 7; Design Centre for the label on p. 89; International Wool Secretariat for the Woolmark and Woolblend symbols on p. 24; Metal Box plc for the information on the history of paper on p. 30; Marks and Spencer plc for the care label on p. 22; Billy Nicholas for the carnival design on p. 69; Procter and Gamble Ltd for the Ariel Automatic packet label on p. 82; Royal Society for the Prevention of Accidents for the BSI information, kitemark and safety mark on p. 7.

Thanks are also due to the following for permission to reproduce photographs: J. Allan Cash pp. 18 (top), 24, 47 (bottom right); Mohamed Ansar Photo Stock Library pp. 52, 70-1; Boots The Chemists p. 38 (baby's chair); Cadbury Schweppes p. 59 (bottom left and right); Christian Aid pp. 18 (bottom left) 22, 34 (top), 44, 46 (top left and bottom), 54 (top), 57 (top); Compix p. 18 (bottom right); Crafts Council p. 53 (centre and bottom); Lesley Garner p. 19 (bottom); Hutchison Library pp. 14, 19 (top right), 28, 57 (bottom);

ICI Films p. 38 (top); Image Bank p. 15 (top left); Imperial War Museum p. 15 (bottom centre); International Institute for Cotton pp. 20-1, 47 (bottom left), 49, 50 (centre), 57 (centre); International Linen p. 33 (top left and right and bottom); International Linen Promotion p. 33 (centre); Lever Bros. pp. 79, 83; London Features International p. 15 (right); Mary Evans Picture Library pp. 15 (top right), 47 (top right), 76; National Plastics p. 38 (bottom right); Pat Novy p. 65; Robert Harding p. 5 (centre and bottom); Rowenta (UK) Ltd p. 86; Royal College of Surgeons p. 62; Science Photo Library p. 38 (top left); Liz Somerville pp. 50 (top and bottom), 51; Topham Picture Library p. 15 (bottom left); Victoria and Albert Museum p. 63; Bob Watkins pp. 38 (bag and apron), 82.

All other photographs supplied by Jenny Ridgwell.

Cartoons by Dave Parkins.
Cartoons on pp. 92-3 by Jonathan Stuart.

Cover illustration by Pat Thorne.
Illustrations by Dataset Marlborough Design, Chris Feely, Maureen and Gordon Gray, and John York.

Contents

Skills in Home Economics: Textiles is the second title in the **Skills in Home Economics** series. Like the first one on food, this book has been written for and tested by lower secondary school pupils. The text is intended to be provocative, creative and demands a variety of skills, leading up to GCSE. Pupils are encouraged to criticise, discuss and evaluate information, and where possible to conduct their own surveys. The text is presented in double-page spreads, with questions, investigations, design problems and further work. Symbols have been used for quick reference, so that pupils and teachers can see at once what type of work or activity is to be done. Most of the questions can be answered using the text, relevant photographs or data, but if other books are required, then this is indicated. The symbols used are as follows:

written work to be done

 needs other books for help

investigative work to look carefully and examine something

 design or invent something yourself

discussion with rest of group and/or teacher

Where possible, authentic up-to-date material has been introduced including newspaper articles and real garment labels.

Cross-curricular material has been deliberately included and consequently pupils will become familiar with pie charts, bar charts and geographical maps.

As before, the text has been occasionally lifted by a funny anecdote and a character called Pinhead has been introduced to reinforce complicated information.

Textiles is an exciting and creative subject area, so colourful design briefs have been set where pupils invent symbols, patterns, puppets and clothing designs. The ultimate design brief is the Notting Hill Carnival and as an example, in 1988 the band Flamingo was followed from original design concept to the final dazzling parade.

The book is intended as a lead into GCSE and Standard Grade and an initiation into the scope and flair of a textiles syllabus.

The authors would like to thank the pupils of Park House Middle School and John Archer School for their help and also Mark, Annabel and Simon Ridgwell for their input. They would also like to thank Sue Walton, the publisher, for her patience and suggestions.

What are textiles and what are they used for?

What is a textile? A good question!

A dictionary will tell you that a textile is 'a woven fabric'. But that means that T-shirt material, which is **knitted**, is not a fabric! Now look up the word 'fabric'. The dictionary says it is 'a manufactured cloth' and 'cloth' is something which 'garments and coverings are made from'!

Today fabrics can be made from so many things. Nearly half of the fibres that we use are made from chemicals. They are known as **man-made fibres**. The rest come from plant and animal sources. Is paper a fabric? Well, it comes from plant fibres – trees actually – and it can be used for garments such as nappies, so yes, why not?

How can textiles be used?

Textiles are not just used for clothes. Look at the pictures below to give you more ideas.

To do

Using the key words to help, write a sentence about each of the pictures, explaining the importance of textiles in each case.

> **Key words**
> waterproof   hold air   strong   flexible
> protective   windproof   warm   colourful

Sails of a surfboard

Hot air balloons

Mountain climbers, dressed for cold weather

5

Textiles used in the home

How can textiles be used around the home?

Questions

1   Look at the picture above and spot the different ways in which textiles have been used in this room. **Remember**, textiles can include paper and plastics.
2   Look around your home or school. Make a list of 10 different ways in which textiles are used. For example, (1) floor coverings,...
3   Choose two ways of using textiles and explain why they are used. Copy the chart below and fill in your answers. One example has been done for you.

Ways of using textiles	Why they are used
door mat	to wipe feet on because it is rough

WIPE

Answer to question 1
(1) floor coverings, (2) fabric curtains, (3) fabric curtain tie back, (4) upholstered chair, (5) newspapers, (6) fabric lampshade, (7) furry teddy, (8) woven carpet, (9) silk flowers, (10) paper wallpaper, (11) cushions, (12) knitted jumper and knitting.

How safe is your home?

In a typical year, 6500 people are killed and 1½ million are injured in home accidents. Fire brigades are called to 58 000 fires in UK homes and 800 people lose their lives in fires each year. **So the home is dangerous!** Fires involving furniture and bedding are the biggest killers as they produce poisonous fumes.

Faulty electric wiring or an accident on the cooker can easily cause a fire in the home

Questions

Look at the article adapted from the *Daily Mail*, January 1988.

1 What was the cause of the fire?
2 What was the 'fatal combination' of materials on the sofa which caught fire?
3 How do you think this blaze might have started?
4 What 'tighter safety rules on furniture' could be introduced?

Three more children killed in sofa blaze

Three children died as a blaze engulfed their home yesterday. The children died in their beds after foam from a settee set alight, filling the house with choking fumes

The tragedy came after Greater Manchester fire chiefs warned of the 'fatal combination' of polyurethane foam and polyester coverings on furniture.

Yesterday's blaze at Stevenage, Hertfordshire, is likely to intensify calls for tighter safety rules on furnishings to cut the dangers of toxic fumes from house fires.

Neighbours said a 'fireball' started in the lounge. They also said they had seen foam stuffing sticking through a hole in the sofa.

Adapted from Daily Mail, January 1988

BSI kitemark and BSI safety mark

British Standards Institution

British Standards set rules and tests for many of the products which might be involved in home accidents. Manufacturers, consumer interests, safety organisations and Government departments are all represented on the BSI committees which draw up the standards. The government often bases safety regulations on these standards.

The familiar BSI kitemark means a product has been made under an approved system of control and testing. Look for it when buying oil heaters, fireguards, pressure cookers, baby harnesses, pushchairs, highchairs and carry cots.

Look for the BSI Safety mark on light fittings, table lamps, cookers, gas fires and water heaters.

BSI kitemark   BSI safety mark

British Standards test many products which are used in the home and likely to be a safety risk.

Use the information on the left to answer the questions.

Questions

1 Name three products which might carry the BSI kitemark.
2 Name three products which might carry the BSI safety mark.
3 Why do you think this type of labelling is important?

Further work

Visit your local Electricity Board Shop or Departmental Store and find three items with a BSI label.

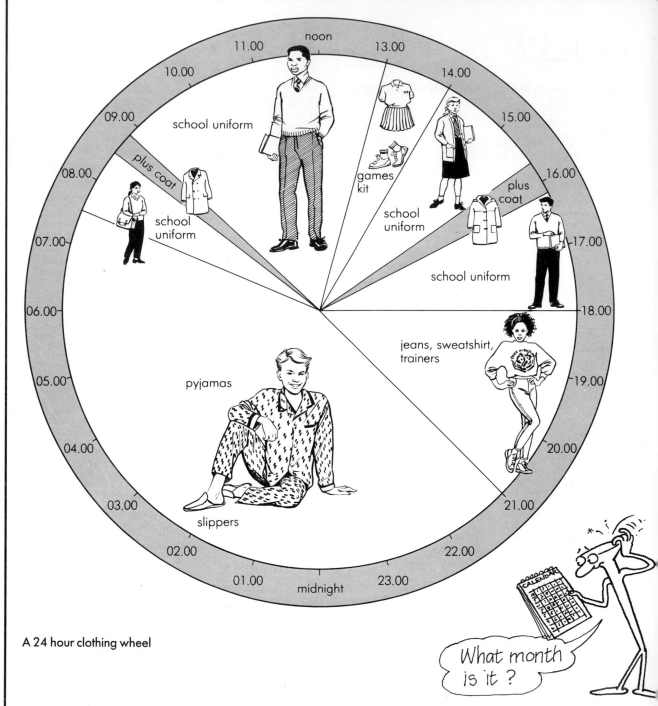

A 24 hour clothing wheel

The types of clothes we choose to wear depend upon many things.

Try to discover some of the reasons why *you* choose your clothes.

To do

Copy the 24 hour clothing wheel. You can trace it or draw your own using a pair of compasses. Fill in the different clothes that you might wear today and the times that you would wear them.

Why did you choose the clothes on the clothing wheel?

To do

Draw up a chart like the one below. Fill in the times and the clothing you wore, giving your reasons for wearing each item.

Time	Clothes worn	Why I chose these clothes
7.30 – 18.00	school uniform	Because I have to!
8.30 – 8.50	coat with school uniform	It's winter so I need a coat to keep warm on the way to school.
13.00 – 14.00	games kit	We have to wear something loose and easy to run around in.
15.40 – 16.10	coat with school uniform	It's still winter!
18.00 – 21.00	jeans, sweatshirt trainers	These are my most comfortable clothes so I can relax in them.
21.00 – 7.30	pyjamas, slippers	Pyjamas are warm and soft for sleeping in. I usually wear slippers indoors.

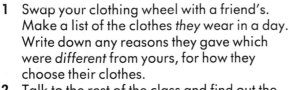

1   Swap your clothing wheel with a friend's. Make a list of the clothes *they* wear in a day. Write down any reasons they gave which were *different* from yours, for how they choose their clothes.
2   Talk to the rest of the class and find out the different reasons for choosing clothes. Write the heading 'How we choose our clothes' and make a list of the reasons you have discovered.
    From your discussions you will have found out that there are many reasons why we choose what we wear.
3   Look at the people on the right. In each case, write down the reasons why their clothes have been chosen.

Many people wear special clothes for work. Some clothing is worn for **protection**. In outer space, spacemen wear special suits with an air supply to help them breathe. Shop assistants sometimes wear **uniforms** so that shoppers can **identify** them if they need help. Nurses and doctors wear **uniforms** to **protect patients** from the **dirt and bacteria** they might carry on their normal clothing.

Dressed for work

To do

Look at the examples of people in working clothes. Choose any *two* people. Copy the chart below and describe why people wear these work clothes. One example has been done for you.

Job	Working clothes	Why they are worn
chef	white overall, neck tie, apron, trousers, white shoes, tall hat	The chef changes completely into clean clothes. These are more hygienic than other clothes. The tall hat stops hair falling onto food. It also tells people who is the chef!

Key words
hard   protection   uniform
identify   fireproof   safety
warm   hygienic   clean
cool

Clothes for sport

1	Motor racing	8	Fencing
2	Horse-riding	9	Football
3	American football	10	Mountaineering
4	Scuba-diving	11	Sailing
5	Swimming	12	Cricket
6	Boxing	13	Skiing
7	Judo	14	Basketball
		15	Gymnastics
		16	Athletics
		17	Ice-hockey

Sports clothes have to be chosen carefully because they need to be **comfortable, easy to wear** and **suitable** for the chosen sport. There are different reasons why we choose special clothes for each activity. Swimwear and leotards are usually made from **stretchy material** so our bodies can move freely. For outdoor activities such as sailing or rockclimbing, we need **warm, protective** clothing.

Coloured clothes help **identify** team members, and **bright colours** help when people need to be **easily seen** when skiing or sailing. In **dangerous** sports, special gear is worn for **safety**. Wicket keepers in cricket wear pads to **protect** their legs, and racing drivers wear **flame resistant** suits, **thick gloves** and **crash helmets**.

To do

Choose *one* of the sportspeople and describe *exactly* what they are wearing. For each item, give a reason why you think they have chosen this clothing. Copy the chart and fill in your own details. An example has been done for you.

Sport	Chosen clothing	What it is made from	Why it is chosen
American football 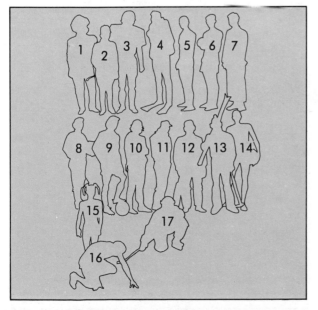	helmet with face protector	a hard material	helmets protect players' heads from injury
	padded coloured shirts	a soft, cotton material with shoulder pads	players have to block others to stop them getting the ball. Big pads make players bigger
	gloves	soft leather	to help with handling the ball
	stretchy pants	stretchy material	running is easy in stretchy material
	socks and shoes	knitted wool, leather	special shoes help to run fast

Question

Imagine that you worked for a sports clothes manufacturer. Design a sports shirt which British athletes could wear at the next Olympics. Draw a picture of your design and suggest what material it could be made from.

A design drawn by Claire Bracken, Park House Middle School

Here is what some pupils thought about fashion.

Is it fashionable?

To do

Begin a class project on 'Fashion'. Find out what people think.
Here is how to start.

1   Write down what you think is meant by the word 'fashion'. Use the key words to help.

> **Key words**
> trendy impress style new young
> different trendsetter unusual fresh
> rebellious shows wealth nice labels

2   Ask two of your friends, 'What is fashion?'. Write down what they think.
3   Use the pictures on page 15. Why might each person be thought to be fashionable? What makes them choose their fashions?

Now as a class discuss your findings.
Display your work as a class project, using posters, computer print out sheets, or folders of your work. Include pictures and written work.

A big problem!

Is fashion important? Can all countries in the world afford to be fashionable? If not, how can we, in the rich countries of the world, change our ideas on fashion?

Question

Can the world afford to be fashionable? Use this picture to give you ideas.

People in famine areas of Ethiopia

Fashion over the world

Clothes

My mother keeps on telling me
When she was in her teens
She wore quite different clothes from mine
And hadn't heard of jeans,

T-shirts, no hats, and dresses that
Reach far above our knees.
I laughed at first and then I thought
One day my kids will tease

And scoff at what I'm wearing now.
What will their fashion be?
I'd give an awful lot to know,
To look ahead and see.

Girls dressed like girls perhaps once more
And boys no longer half
Resembling us. Oh, what's in store
To make our children laugh?

Elizabeth Jennings

Questions

Read through the poem by Elizabeth Jennings.
1   Name three pieces of clothing which the writer's mother did not wear as a teenager.
2   How does the writer think that boys and girls will dress in the future?
3   Make up a short poem about the clothes that you wear.

To do

1   Draw and label an outfit which you could wear for:
    (a) a disco, (b) a trip to Mars.
    Which of these outfits is fashionable? Why?
2   In your own words, explain why you think fashions in clothes change.
3   Ask some older people in your area what they wore as teenagers. Perhaps they could show you some photographs. Ask them why they chose these clothes, where they bought them from and why they liked them. How much have fashions changed since those times?

What a tip!

Clothes need looking after if they are to look nice. Does this room remind you of anybody's that you know?

Questions

1 How could the room in the picture be tidied up? Make a list of all the ways that you can think of and compare your list with the rest of the group.
2 Draw a picture or describe how you look after the clothes in your room. What improvements could you make?

Textile wordsearch

In the wordsearch there are 20 words which all have something to do with textiles and their properties – words such as **soft**, **fluffy**, and **fine**. Make a list of as many as you can find. From your list choose three words to describe fabrics for: (a) nappies, (b) tent material, (c) swimming costumes.

```
T B L S T R E T C H Y
H A C M C L I N G Y F
I N C O M F O R T P I
C A C O O L U R E M R
K R E T S U F I N E M
L I G H T F A D B R E
P O W A R F S S R S L
U H A I R Y S T O Y A
S T R O N G H I S F S
V I M L E R M F B A T
R C R E A S E F A S I
S A L P R O T E C T C
```

Cloth into clothing

All around the world, clothes can be made using simple rectangles of fabric. These pictures show how cloth can be wound round the body to make a garment or head dress. In **hot** climates, **light, cotton fabrics** are used. People who live in **colder climates** wear **warmer fabrics** such as **wool**.

Fabrics are, of course, used to make more complicated garments with sleeves, darts and fitted trousers. Most of the people in the pictures are also wearing garments which need to be sewn together. The ladies wearing the saris are also wearing fitted tops which match the colour and design of the sari.

Three girls in saris

A Buddhist monk

Lesotho capes

Scotsman
with kilt

Mali lady

Arab boys wearing turbans

Questions

1 Choose one of the people in the photos and show, using a drawing, how a length of fabric has been used to make a garment.
2 Design a garment for yourself using one length of fabric. Draw a picture of yourself wearing your design.
3 What other clothes can you think of which use straight lengths of fabric?

Further work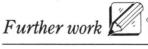

Find out more about one of the following:
(a) saris, (b) Scottish tartans, (c) kimonos, (d) what Buddhist monks wear.
Write up what you find out. Include some pictures with your work.

Nearly half the textiles used in the world are made from **cotton**. The cotton in the clothes we wear comes from the **cotton plant**.

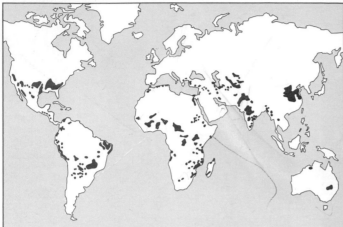

Map showing cotton-growing areas of the world

Cotton picking in Iran

1 Cotton is produced in 80 countries around the world between latitudes 45° North and 30° South. Cotton grows in dry, semi-humid areas.

2 On small farms, whole families help with the cotton harvesting by picking the ripe **cotton bolls**.

Cotton seeds, cotton boll, raw cotton fibre

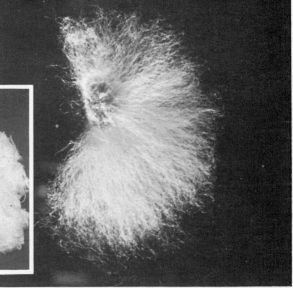

Cotton seed with cotton fibre

3 When cotton bolls are harvested, the **seeds** are removed and used for cooking oils and margarine. The raw cotton is ready for making **textiles**.

4 Every cotton boll contains about 30 seeds, each with a tuft of raw cotton attached. The raw **fibre** has to be **separated** from the seed by a process called **ginning**.

At the **spinning mill** the **cotton fibres** are sorted, then drawn into thick rope and **spun** and **twisted** into **yarn**.

```
              drawn           drawn        spun
                                          twisted
cotton fibres → soft, thick rope → thinner rope → yarn
```

Processing cotton

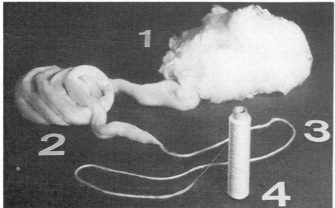

Cotton fibres in four different states

Cotton cloth can be **woven** or **knitted** by machine. When it comes off the loom it is in a 'grey' state. Before it is coloured and printed it needs to be **bleached** and **cleaned**.

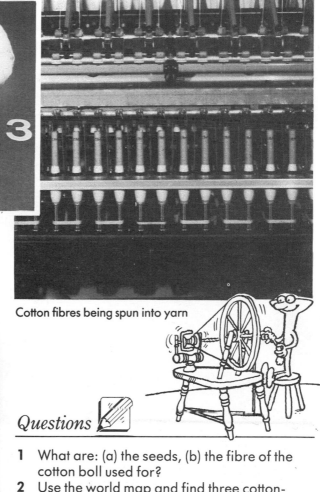

Cotton fibres being spun into yarn

Cotton cloth from the loom in the 'grey' state

Questions

1 What are: (a) the seeds, (b) the fibre of the cotton boll used for?
2 Use the world map and find three cotton-producing countries.
3 What happens to the cotton fibre after it is harvested?

Further work

Start a project on 'The History of Cotton'

Find out where cotton came from, the history of the Industrial Revolution, the cotton mills, the slave trade and inventors such as Richard Arkwright, who invented the spinning machine, also Eli Whitney, who invented the cotton gin.

ﾑ

More about cotton

Properties of cotton

Cotton has some very useful properties.

Property	Why this property is useful
• Cotton easily absorbs water.	This makes cotton pleasant and comfortable to wear and allows skin to breathe.
• Cotton fibres are very strong.	Even the lightest fabrics wear well and last a long time.
• Cotton can be boiled and washed in hot water without spoiling the fibres.	This makes cotton easy to keep clean.
• Chemicals can be used on cotton without harming it.	Chemicals can make cotton crease resistant, shrink resistant, coloured, glazed, water repellant and it can even be treated with chemicals so it does not burn.

Tribesmen

Questions

1 Why do people wear cotton clothes in hot climates?
2 Why is cotton easy to keep clean?
3 Name three ways in which cotton can be treated with chemicals.

Questions

Look at the two labels.
1 Draw the symbol for cotton. Why do you think this shape is chosen?
2 What is the difference between the washing instructions for the two garments?
3 Guess the identity of each garment — what clues are you given?
4 What other language is used on the 'St Michael' label? Why is it used?

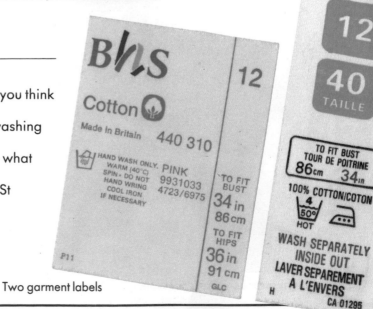

Two garment labels

Page 22

Where cotton grows

Where is cotton produced around the world? Look at the **pie chart** below which shows the countries which produce the most cotton in the world. A pie chart is divided into **sectors**. Each sector is like a **slice of an apple pie**. Whoever gets the biggest slice of the pie has the most!

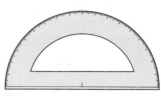

Use a protractor to measure angles

Angle

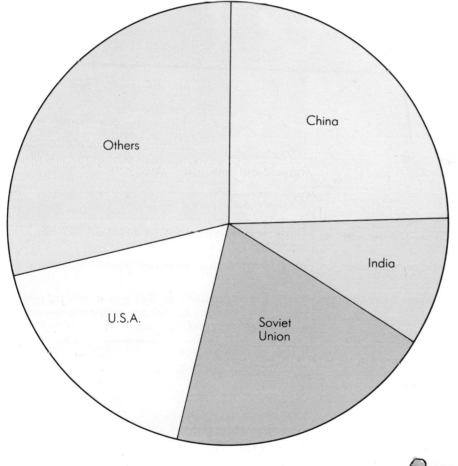

Pie chart to show the world cotton-producing areas

Question

List, in order, the cotton-producing areas of the world, starting with the country that produces the most – that is, the largest sector of the pie chart.

You may need to measure the exact angle at the centre of the circle of some sectors, using a protractor.

23

Wool is the **fibre** from the **soft coat** of a **sheep**. Each coat of wool is called a **fleece** and this is **sheared** from the sheep, using **clippers**. The fleece is cleaned and processed before being turned into cloth for clothes, carpets and blankets.

A sheep and lamb

Properties of wool

Wool has some useful properties.

Property	Why this property is useful
• Wool is soft, comfortable and warm.	This makes wool an ideal fibre for clothes and blankets, especially in colder climates.
• Wool is hardwearing and water does not soak into it easily.	Wool makes beautiful, long-lasting carpets.
• Wool does not burn easily or catch fire – instead it chars.	Wool garments can save lives. Racing car drivers and people who work in jobs with a high fire risk, wear protective clothing made from wool.

The Woolmark symbol

The Woolmark symbol on a fabric or yarn means that it is made from pure new wool, and that it has met the quality and performance standards laid down by the International Wool Secretariat.

The **Woolblendmark** means that an item bearing the mark has been made from a minimum of 60% new wool, blended with other fibres.

CERTIFICATION TRADE MARK
PURE NEW WOOL

The Woolmark

CERTIFICATION TRADE MARK
WOOL RICH BLEND

The Woolblendmark

Wool questions

1 Copy the sentences below and fill in the gaps using the text to help.
The ... of the sheep is ... using clippers. After cleaning and spinning, wool can be made into ... and ... . In cold climates woollen clothes keep us ... .
2 Why is wool a useful fibre to use for:
(a) blankets, (b) carpets, (c) clothes for racing drivers?
3 Why do you think the shape of the Woolmark symbol has been chosen?
4 What is the difference between the Woolmark symbol and the Woolblendmark?
5 Design your own symbol for a piece of clothing made of wool.

Symbols designed by Alistair

Further work

Start a project on wool. Here are some ideas. Make a list of all the things that you can think of which are made of wool. Try to think of reasons why wool has been chosen for *three* of those items.

Find out more about different breeds of sheep and which breed produces the best wool. How does wool from a sheep become a jumper or carpet?

Conduct a survey to find out how many of your clothes are made from wool.

Woollen clothes

These two care labels are found on clothes made from wool.

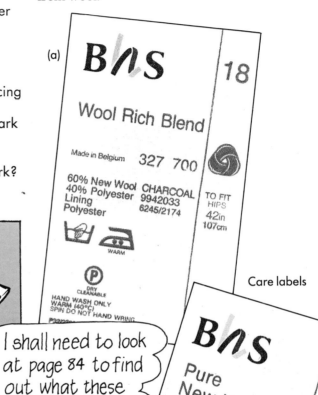

Care labels

I shall need to look at page 84 to find out what these drawings mean.

Questions

1 Which garment, (a) or (b), is made completely from wool?
2 What is the other garment made from? How do you know this?
3 How should each garment be washed?
4 What sort of garment do you think each label belongs to?

1 In Britain there are more than 35 million sheep. These include more than 40 different **hill**, **mountain** and **downland** breeds.

The farmers need to sell the wool for the best price they can. To help them do this, the Government set up the **British Wool Marketing Board**, in 1950.

2 There are about 93 000 farmers, who produce 40 million kg (or 40 000 tonnes) of **fleece wool** every year.

3 The **average size** of a flock of sheep is 230. They need to be **shorn** annually.

4 The wool is collected by one of the British Wool Marketing Board's **handling merchants**. Then it is **graded** and got ready for **auction.**

5 There are 24 sales during the year, where the wool is auctioned to the **wool trade**. Eight of these sales are held in Edinburgh, and the other 16 are held at the Board's head office in Bradford.

6 After the auction, the wool is taken to a **scouring plant**.

7 At the scouring plant the wool is washed. This removes most of the **grease, oil**, and other **impurities**.

8 Next the wool is **combed** or **carded**. This makes all the fibres line up in the same direction.

9 After this, the wool is **spun**. There are different processes, depending on what the wool is to be used for.

10 The yarns can now be used for making things such as **knitwear**, **carpets**, **tweeds** and **hand-knitting wools**.

Woolly quiz

Look at the chart.
1 How many sheep farmers and sheep are there in Britain?
What is the average size of flock?
2 Explain how wool is removed from a sheep.
3 What happens when wool is:
(a) graded, (b) auctioned, (c) scoured?
4 Why must wool be combed or carded?
5 Name *four* ways of using wool yarn.

11 Over 60% of British wool is exported **unprocessed**, as fleece wool, or **semi-processed**, after it is scoured. It is sold to more than 50 countries, all over the world.

Tear a piece of newspaper and you will see that the edge is made up of many tiny **fibres**. Paper is made by **matting** these fibres together into **sheets** to make a valuable textile which can be used in many different ways.

The history of paper

Paper maker in Korea using bamboo frame

History

Around 3000 BC the Egyptians made the first paper-like material for writing from reeds called papyrus. However, it was the Chinese in the first century AD who made the first real paper. It was made from the bark of mulberry trees, old fishing nets and waste hemp, which were beaten into a pulp. The mixture was then put on a bamboo mat and left to drain. After drying it was peeled off and used as writing paper.

In the 12th century AD paper was being made in Europe, and the first British paper mill was founded in Stevenage in 1490. Up to the end of the 18th century paper was made from rags, and during that century small boxes were also made.

Early in the 19th century wood became the raw material used for paper making. Paper then became cheap enough to be used as a common packaging material.

Courtesy Metal Box plc

New and recycled paper

All paper is made from **vegetable fibres**, in particular **wood**. These fibres are **pulped**, **beaten**, then **matted together** as paper. Paper can be used over and over again. **Recycled paper** saves valuable trees from being chopped down.

Waste paper from newspapers or magazines has to be cleaned and sorted before it can be pulped and **recycled** into paper for packaging materials such as egg boxes, or used for newspaper. In the UK 52% of paper pulp is made from waste paper.

Questions

Look at the flow chart on p.29.
1 Describe in your own words how paper is made.
2 Make a list of all the different ways in which you have already used paper today. For example, you may have read a newspaper or used some loo paper!
3 Wander round your school and make a list of different ways that paper and cardboard are used – for example posters and books.
4 Now imagine that paper did not exist. Describe a day at school – remember this book would not exist either!

How is paper made?

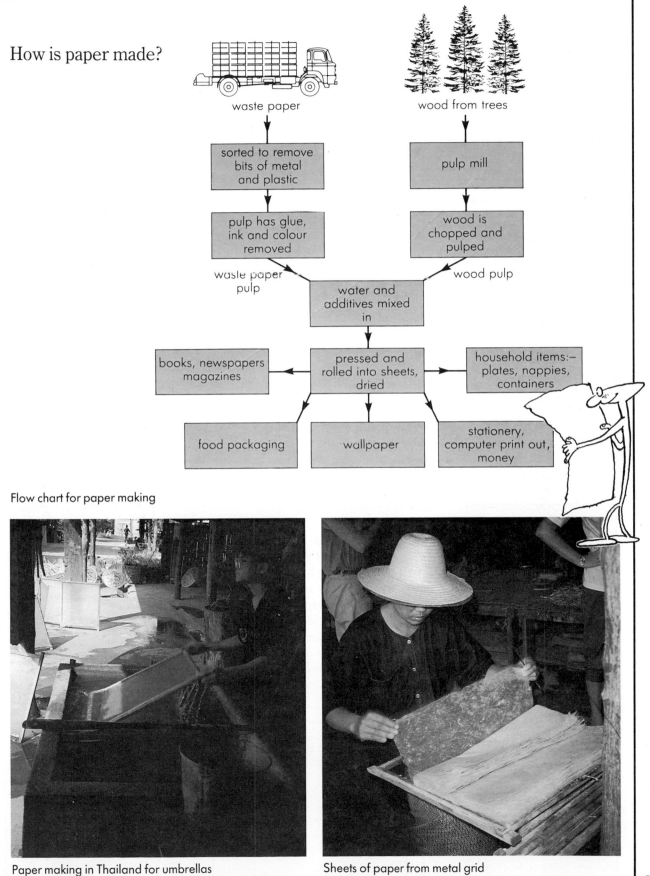

waste paper

wood from trees

sorted to remove bits of metal and plastic

pulp mill

pulp has glue, ink and colour removed

wood is chopped and pulped

waste paper pulp

wood pulp

water and additives mixed in

books, newspapers magazines

pressed and rolled into sheets, dried

household items:— plates, nappies, containers

food packaging

wallpaper

stationery, computer print out, money

Flow chart for paper making

Paper making in Thailand for umbrellas

Sheets of paper from metal grid

Recycled paper

Make your own recycled paper

You can use torn up scraps of coloured or used newspaper to make your own sheet of paper.
You need: a large bowl, a measuring jug, warm water, scraps of used paper (cartridge paper works well), a processor or liquidizer, a piece of fine wire gauze about 15 cm square (the sort used to repair cars), 2 J-cloths, a rolling pin, an iron.

What to do

1 Half fill the bowl with warm water. Tear up scraps of used paper and put them in the bowl. Leave to soak for 10 minutes – longer if possible.

2 Pour a little of this paper and water into the processor and whizz until smooth (about 20-30 seconds). Repeat until all the scrap paper has been pulped.

3 Pour it back into the bowl. Carefully dip the gauze into the bowl, tipping it until the gauze is evenly coated with the sludgy mixture.

4 Hold the gauze over the bowl and let the water drip out.

5 Place the gauze on one J-cloth and then cover it with another. Roll it over with a rolling pin to squeeze out excess water.

6 Turn it over and remove the piece of gauze. You can make more sheets of paper later. Your piece of wet paper is now sandwiched between the two J-cloths.

7 Iron with a warm iron until the paper begins to dry. This can take a few minutes.

8 Slowly peel off the top cloth and remove the handmade paper. Leave it to dry for one day in a warm place.

Household waste

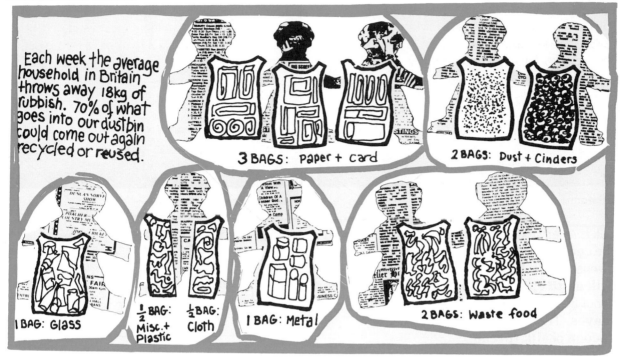

Each week the average household in Britain throws away 18kg of rubbish. 70% of what goes into our dustbin could come out again recycled or reused.

3 BAGS: paper + card

2 BAGS: Dust + Cinders

1 BAG: Glass

½ BAG: Misc.+ Plastic

½ BAG: Cloth

1 BAG: Metal

2 BAGS: Waste food

Household waste

To do

1 Make a list of the different rubbish thrown into British dustbins.
2 Why recycle?
   'Recycling is an important part of conservation and needs to be tackled worldwide.' This sentence comes from a Christian Aid leaflet. Work in small groups and discuss why it is important to recycle and reuse waste products, especially paper. Write down two reasons that your group thinks are important. As a class, sort these reasons into order, starting with the most important. Display your work as a poster, with the heading 'Recycling waste'.
3 How could you organize a collection of used paper in your area? Ask your local council about paper collection or a waste paper merchant.

The harvest of Manila

In the developing world vast urban shanty towns have grown up beside the rapidly expanding cities. Some of the poorest shanty town dwellers earn a living by harvesting, not from the land, but from the streets and rubbish tips of the cities.

Manila, the capital city of the Philippines, is such a city. In one of the slum areas of the city is a huge rubbish dump known as Smoky Mountain. It is a dangerous and unhealthy place but for some collecting rubbish is the only way they have of making a living.

Many of the 'harvesters' form teams of family groups and collect, sort and sell what they find to middlemen, who re-sell for re-use or recycling, usually at a vast profit. They may bring in a harvest of paper, tins, glass, material, bones, plastic...

Courtesy Christian Aid

Questions

1 What 'harvest' do the poor people of Manila gather from the rubbish tips?
2 What happens to this 'harvest'?

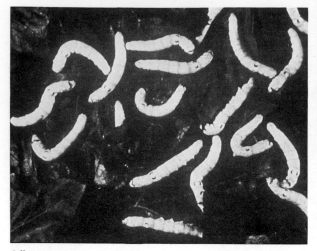
Silkworms

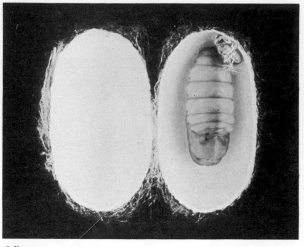
Silkworm cocoons

Silk is a very expensive fabric which comes from the **cocoon** spun around the **silkworm**. Thousands of silkworms are bred on **silk farms**. **Silk moth** eggs hatch into **silkworms** and for about five weeks a silkworm eats **mulberry leaves**. Then it stops eating, and spins a **cocoon** of **silk thread**.

Silkworms would soon turn into moths and break this thread, so they have to be killed. The silk thread is then wound from the cocoon onto a reel. Nearly 1000 metres of thread comes from one cocoon. These silk threads are twisted to make thicker yarn suitable for weaving.

Silk is a strong, soft, **lustrous** fabric. It can be made into dresses, ties and underwear. The wedding dress of the Princess of Wales was made from silk taffeta.

Questions

1 Make a large copy of the flow chart to show how silk fabric is made. Sort each of the phrases below into order then fit them on the flow diagram.
- silkworm stops eating and spins cocoon
- eggs hatch into silkworms
- silkworm killed and silk taken from cocoon
- silkworm feeds for five weeks
2 Why do you think silk is an expensive fabric?
3 List *five* items which could be made from silk.

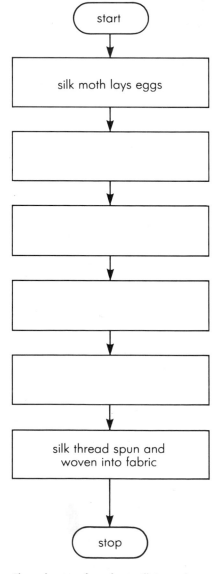

Flow chart to show how silk is made

start → silk moth lays eggs → → → → silk thread spun and woven into fabric → stop

Harvesting flax

Flax plants in flower

Linen is the oldest textile in the world. It is made from the stem of the **flax** plant. Flax has small blue or white flowers. The **long fibres** from the stem are **spun** into linen yarn and then **woven** into linen **fabric**.

Linen can be used for clothing, furnishing fabrics, tea towels, string and rope.

The rest of the flax plant is used for:
- linseed oil for paints,
- plasterboard and paper,
- animal feed.

The properties of linen

Advantages   cool, comfortable, strong and long lasting
Disadvantages   creases and crumples, expensive.

Quick quiz

1   What is linen made from?
2   What is linen used for?
3   How can the rest of the plant be used?

Linen clothes

Linen trade mark

Animal hairs

In different parts of the world, animal hairs are used to make garments. Soft, fluffy **mohair** comes from the fleece of the **angora goat**, which also gives us the yarn **angora**. The long, white hairs of the **angora rabbit** are used to make **angora** too. **Cashmere** is the luxurious hair from the undercoat of the **cashmere goat**, which lives in the mountainous areas of Northern India. The **llama** from South America is related to the camel and produces **alpaca** hair, a fine, soft fibre which is tough and strong like the animal. Alpaca is used for jumpers and blankets. The hair from the **Bactrian camel** of central Asia makes **camel hair cloth**, used for overcoats.

A llama

Leather

Prehistoric people used the skins of animals for clothing, footwear and to make shelters such as tents. People learned to **treat** the **raw hide** with **chemicals** to prevent it from **decaying** and to change the **colour** and **texture**. This process which changes the hide into leather is known as **tanning**.

Boat made from leather

Questions

1 Which goats give their name to a soft yarn?
2 Which *two* animals produce angora?
3 Name *two* types of camel hair and what they are used for.
4 Find out what: (a) mohair, (b) angora, (c) cashmere can be used for.
5 Why do raw hides need to be tanned to make leather?

6 Make a list of as many items as you can think of which can be made from leather. Compare your list with other class members to see who has found the most.
7 What fabrics can be used instead of leather for the following items: (a) car seats, (b) shoes, (c) bags?

What are man-made fibres?

In 1664, Robert Hooke, a British scientist, suggested that it might be possible to copy the way a silkworm spins thread from its body.

In the 1820s Sir Joseph Swann was trying to find a fibre which he could use for a filament in light bulbs. He made **cellulose threads** from **vegetables**. He was rather cross to find that his children had woven them into table mats, but realized that he had invented a new kind of textile.

Sir Joseph Swann invents a new fibre

A silkworm disease struck France during the 1850s and scientists such as Louis Pasteur and Comte Hilaire de Chardonnet discovered a replacement for silk using vegetable fibres and chemicals. This artificial silk was later called **viscose rayon** (and sometimes **rayon** or **viscose**).

Textile manufacturers continued to experiment and develop better ways of producing this fibre and today viscose rayon is used to make many different kinds of material.

Questions

1 Describe how viscose rayon was invented.
2 Using the flow chart, write *three* sentences to explain how viscose rayon is made.
3 When viscose rayon is made, how has the way a silkworm spins thread from its body been copied?

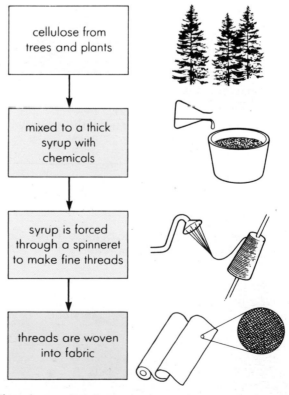

cellulose from trees and plants

↓

mixed to a thick syrup with chemicals

↓

syrup is forced through a spinneret to make fine threads

↓

threads are woven into fabric

Flow chart to show how rayon is made

Man-made fibres are not just used for everyday clothing. They are also used for protective clothing (for example, firemen's suits), home textiles, floor coverings, medical and surgical products, transport, computers, cables, ropes, space travel and agriculture.

Some of the things that man-made fibres are used for

Fibres made from chemicals

Other fibres known as '**man-made**' or **synthetic** fibres can be made from chemicals. Liquids are squirted through tiny holes (**spinnerets**) and when they meet the air they set, forming a thread.

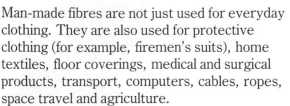

To do

Here are the names of some of these fibres. Can you find them in the wordsearch?

acrylic	lycra	polyester
courtelle	crimplene	tricel
nylon	acrilan	terylene
viscose	orlon	

```
V E X E Y N L E N E
T B A C R Y L I C E
E R B D R L Y C R A
R V I S C O S E I C
Y O M C R N Y O M R
L O R N E I T E P I
E R Y L Y L L O L L
N Y L L O B A T E A
E S A I T N B O N N
S P O L Y E S T E R
C O U R T E L L E Y
```

The advantages of man-made fibres

Man-made fibres have many good properties.

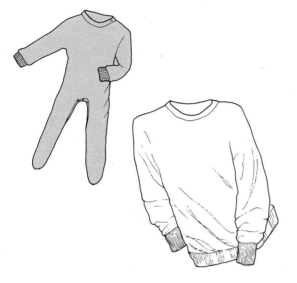

The advantages of man-made fibres

Question

Give *three* properties which are important for:
a) duvet covers   c) underwear,
   or sheets,   d) carpets,
b) shirts,   e) nightwear.

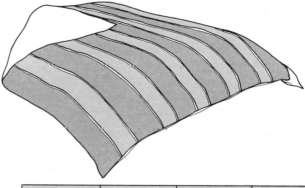

long lasting	stretchy	soft	comfortable
lightweight	resist stains	easy-care	less ironing
warm	resist fire	supporting	bright colours

Questions

The bar chart shows the **world consumption** (use) of different fibres.
Use the bar chart and information on this page to answer the questions.

1 Which fibre is used most for fabrics? How far behind is the second kind of fibre? Why do you think the difference is so small?
2 What fibres might come under the heading 'man-made'?
3 Why do you think that less wool is used, compared with cotton and man-made fibres?

What's a bar chart?

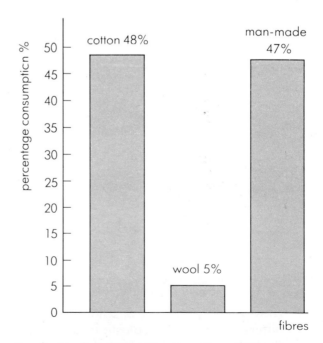

Bar chart to show the world consumption of different fibres

Plastics can be used for many everyday things such as clothing, toys, food packaging and toothbrushes, yet plastics have been widely produced for only thirty years.

Everyday plastics

This helmet is made from polypropylene and is very strong.

Safety helmet

A sailboard

These sails are made of polyester fibre and polyester film. They are strong, waterproof and flexible.

The seat of this high chair is covered with PVC-coated fabric to make it easy to clean and hygienic.

Using PVC

The shopping bag and apron are both coated with PVC (polyvinylchloride) to make them waterproof.

A baby's highchair

Future plastics

Scientists are constantly developing new uses for plastics. Kelvar, a light fabric which does not burn, is used to make bullet-proof jackets.

A bullet-proof jacket

Questions

1 Look around your home or school and list ten different ways in which plastic is used – even this book is covered in a type of plastic!

2 Find out more about the use of plastics. Use books or leaflets from companies who make plastics.

How can you find out what fibres a fabric is made from?

Most garments have **care labels** which tell you what fibres have been used. It is very difficult to judge a fibre just by feeling it. One simple test is to burn the fabric.

Take care! Fire can be dangerous.

To do: burning test

This test should only be conducted under the supervision of a teacher. Pieces of burning fabric are hot and dangerous.
You need: a pair of long tongs, a flameproof tray such as a baking tray, matches (or you can use the flame of a gas burner or bunsen burner), small samples of fabric or thread – choose cotton, wool, synthetic materials and some that you can't identify.

What to do

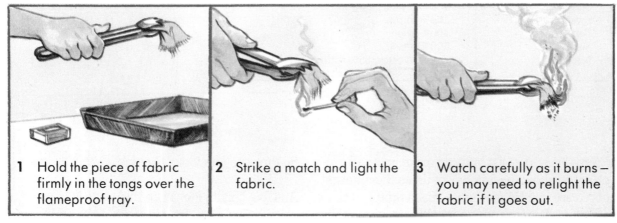

1 Hold the piece of fabric firmly in the tongs over the flameproof tray.

2 Strike a match and light the fabric.

3 Watch carefully as it burns – you may need to relight the fabric if it goes out.

What happens?
Copy the chart below and fill in the details for three of the fabrics you tested.

What happens during burning?	fabric 1	fabric 2	fabric 3
What does the flame look like? Does the fabric burn with lots of smoke or does it smoulder?			
Does it burn easily?			
What does it smell like?			
What was left at the end?			

What should happen
Animal fibres such as wool and silk burn slowly, giving off the smell of burnt hair. A black ash is left.

Vegetable fibres such as cotton and linen burn rapidly, smell like burning paper and leave very little ash.
Synthetic fibres such as nylon and polyester burn rapidly and melt to a hard bead.

What are your clothes made from?

Dominic, a second year pupil, made a list of his
clothes and what they were made from.

Garment	Fabric
Coat	100% wool
Trousers	50% polyester, 40% wool, 10% acrylic
Cords	100% cotton
Tracksuit	69% cotton, 31% polyester
Trousers	65% wool, 35% polyester
Trousers	65% polyester, 35% viscose
Trousers	100% polyester
Stretch jeans	98% cotton, 2% polyurethane
Shorts	100% cotton
Jumper	50% cotton, 50% acrylic
Jumper	100% wool
Jumper	100% acrylic
Jumper	65% wool, 35% polyester
T-shirt	100% cotton
Shirt	65% polyester, 35% cotton
Shirt	100% cotton
Sweatshirt	100% cotton
Pants	100% nylon
Socks	100% cotton
Nightwear	65% polyester, 35% cotton

From this sort of list you can make up a **tally
chart** to show the number of times the different
fibres are used in garments. Each time you count
a fibre such as cotton, you make a tally mark like
this. /

So three counts looks like this. ///

And five counts looks like this. ⦸

Draw up a tally chart and then fill it in.

Tally chart

Type of fibre	Tally of number of times used	Count
wool	//	2
mixed fibres – (for example cotton/polyester)	⦸ /////	9
cotton	⦸ /	6
one man made fibre only – polyester or acrylic or nylon.	///	3
	Total count	20

At the end, check that the total count (in this
case 20) is the same as the number of garments
in the chart.

Now you can draw a bar chart from these results.

Bar charts

A **bar chart** is a simple way of showing
information. Here are some simple rules for
drawing bar charts.
- A bar chart must have a heading.
- The two axes (lines going up and across the
  page) must be labelled.
- Draw the chart carefully using a pencil and
  ruler.
- Each bar must be the same width and should
  be labelled.
- You can colour in the bars if you like.

Questions

1 Look at the bar chart. Which type of fibre in
   this survey was: (a) the most popular, (b) the
   least popular?
2 Why do you think so many clothes are made
   from mixed fibres?

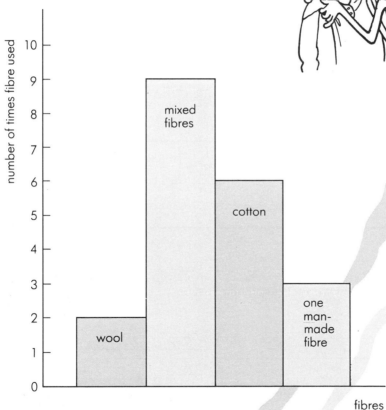

Bar chart to show the different fibres used in Dominic's clothes

Further work

Make a list of your own clothes and use the
labels to find out what they are made from.
Choose between 10 and 20 items. Make a tally
chart, like the one shown on page 40, and then
draw a bar chart. Compare your bar chart with
those of other members of the class. Which is the
most popular fibre? To find out you could draw
up a large bar chart to show the results from the
class.

Fabric puzzles

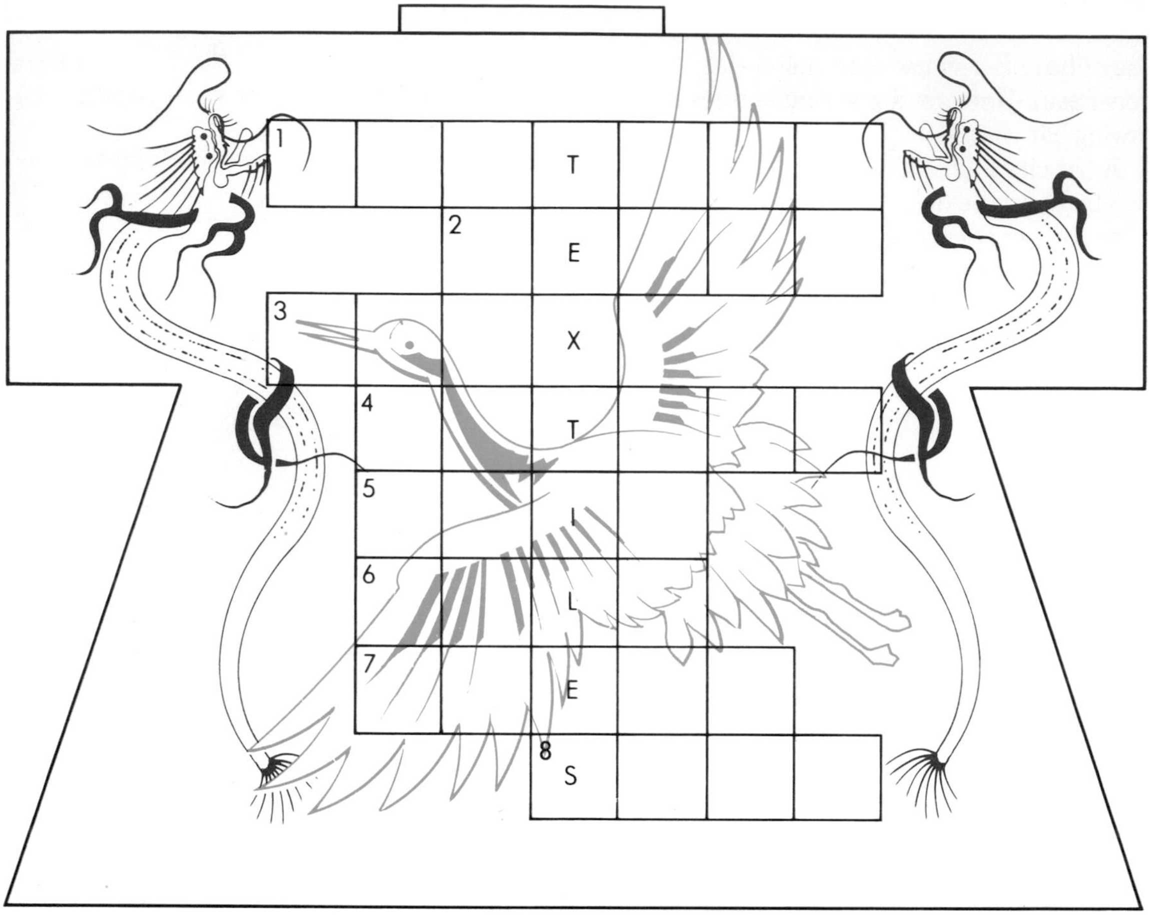

Textile quiz

Fill in each of the answers to the quiz.

1 What fabric is made from animal skins?
2 A loom is used to – – – – – threads to make fabrics.
3 What plant is used to make linen?
4 What fluffy plant makes a cool fabric, suitable for hot weather?
5 Two needles and some wool are used to – – – – a jumper.
6 This fabric is made by tiny animals who eat mulberry leaves.
7 What animals give us wool?
8 We – – – – wool to twist it into thread.

Final question

What is the garment around the crossword puzzle called and what country does it come from?

Answer
Kimono, from Japan

Fibre link up

These plants, animals or chemicals can be useful for making the fibres and fabrics listed here.

Fibres and fabrics
paper   angora   rope   linen   cotton   wool
alpaca   cashmere   man-made fibres
camel hair   silk

Sheep

Cotton boll

Camel

Trees

Silkworm

Llama

Chemicals

Rabbit

Jute

Flax

Goat

Questions

1 Make a list to show the link between the pictures and the fibres and fabrics. For example,
   • silkworm – silk
2 Choose *three* of the fibres and describe what they can be used for.

Answers
cotton boll – cotton; trees – paper; silkworm – silk;
rabbit – angora; jute – rope; flax – linen; sheep –
wool; llama – alpaca; goat – cashmere; chemicals –
man-made fibre; camel – camel hair

Fibres such as cotton, wool or polyester can be **spun** or **twisted** into **yarns**. These yarns can then be **woven**, **knitted** or used in other ways to make **fabrics**.

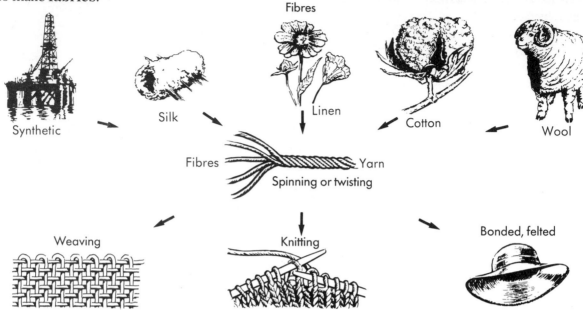

Fibres

Synthetic

Silk

Linen

Cotton

Wool

Fibres — Spinning or twisting — Yarn

Weaving

Knitting

Bonded, felted

The stages in production of fabrics

Natural fibres such as wool or cotton are usually short, so they have to be **twisted** into yarn.

Chemically made fibres such as nylon are made in a **continuous filament** (thread) and may be very long. Sometimes these filaments are cut and spun, like natural fibres.

Carding and spinning

Fluffy fibres from the cotton plant or wools and hairs have to be **untangled** before they can be spun into yarn. In earlier times, **teasel heads**, a type of prickly thistle, were used. The Romans called the teasel *carduus*, which gives us the word **carding** by which we mean **untangling fibres**.

Natural fibres are short and fine so they need to be **twisted** into a yarn before they can be used for weaving or knitting. This twisting process is called **spinning**.

Mali women spinning cotton

For hundreds of years, cotton and wool have been spun by hand. Hand spinning produces a slightly uneven yarn which can't be made by machines.

In factories, complicated machinery, often controlled by computers, can spin and twist fibres at great speed into yarns for weaving and knitting.

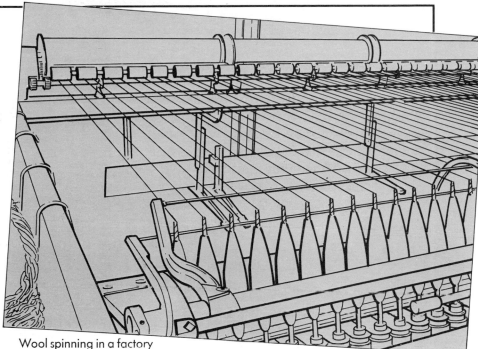

Wool spinning in a factory

To do: *try your hand at spinning*

You need: a cotton wool ball – the sort used in first aid boxes.
(Did you know that the cotton wool ball is not made of cotton? Try the burning test on page 39 to find out what fibre is used.)

You can judge the yarns by measuring to find the **longest**. One class produced a yarn 1½ metres in length. **But** yarn should also be **evenly twisted**. Lumpy yarn is poor quality because it breaks when it is knitted or spun.

What to do
1 Hold the cotton wool ball in one hand. Use the finger and thumb of the other hand to pull and twist the fibres gently into a yarn.
2 Sometimes licking your fingers helps with the twisting! Try and make a long, even yarn.
3 Which member of the class has made the best yarn?

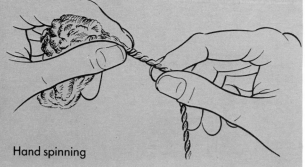

Hand spinning

Questions

1 Write a sentence to explain the term 'carding'.
2 What could you use your cotton wool yarn for? Try out your idea.

3 Name *two* fibres which need to be spun.
4 Use other books to find then draw a picture of a spinning wheel. Explain briefly how a spinning wheel works.

Many fabrics are made by weaving together **two sets of threads**. The threads which run down the fabric are called the **warp threads**. **Weft threads**, which run across, are woven across the warp threads. Fabrics can be woven on **looms**. The loom is first threaded with warp threads then the **weaver** threads the weft thread across the warp to make the fabric.

A weaver from the Karen Hill Tribe in Thailand

Bolivian weavers using a loom

Looms can be very simple, like these wooden frames used by Bolivian weavers. They are working outside and making cloth for rugs or wrap-over garments.

This weaver has part of her loom tied around her waist to help keep the weaving in shape. She comes from the Karen Hill Tribe in Thailand and is weaving **jute** into pink cloth for tribal costume. The thread which she weaves across the fabric is simply wound round a stick.

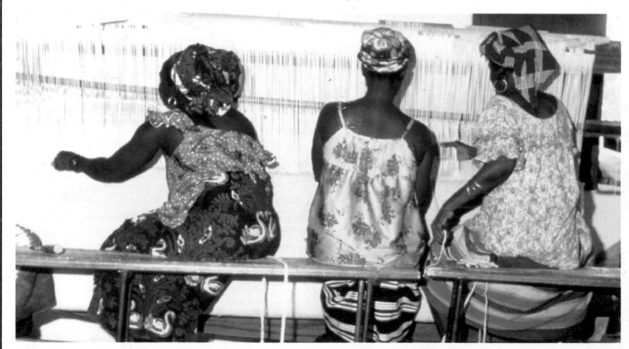

Weaving a carpet, in Mali

This carpet loom is constructed out of wood. Three weavers are working at making this carpet, in Mali, West Africa.

Weaving silk, in Northern Thailand

An 18th century loom

This silk weaver works at a factory visited by the Princess of Wales, in Northern Thailand. Notice the many blue silk warp threads on this weaver's loom. She pushes the shuttle backwards and forwards across these threads as she weaves lengths of hand-made silk cloth – a very expensive fabric!

Handwoven cloth takes time to make. With so many people in the world needing clothes, it was necessary to speed up the weaving process. In the 18th century during the **Industrial Revolution** in Britain, looms were being used in the north of England. At first they were driven by steam, then later by electricity.

Computer-controlled weaving

Peruvian mother and children in woven and knitted clothes

In factories today, the skill of the weaver has been overtaken by the computer. This loom is a very complex piece of machinery. The picture shows orange and blue warp threads. The shuttle on the left hand side can even wind itself some more thread! It then speeds backwards and forwards across the warp threads, automatically weaving the cloth.

Questions

1 Choose two of the looms in the pictures. Describe how the looms might be got ready for weaving and how the weaving might be done.
2 Which method of weaving do you like best? Explain why.

To do

Try some simple weaving
using strips of paper.

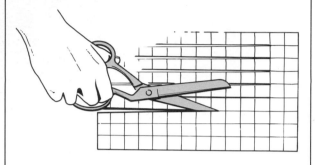

1 Cut a piece of squared paper into 1 cm wide strips. Leave a gap of 3 cm uncut at the top. These strips are called the **warp.**

2 Cut coloured paper into strips. These strips are called the **weft.**

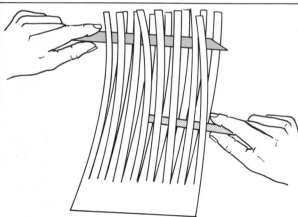

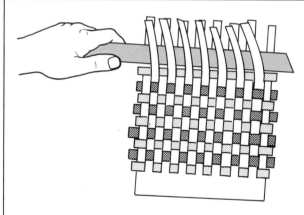

3 Lift up **every other** warp strip. Use a ruler to help. Weave in the coloured **weft** strip.

4 Now lift up the next set of warp strips. Weave in another coloured weft strip. Repeat until the squared paper is fully woven. You have just made a **plain** weave.

To do

1 Look at the picture on the right for the twill weave. Use another piece of squared paper and coloured strips. Try making a twill weave.

2 Invent your own weave and give it a name, using another piece of squared paper and strips. How strong is your weave? Do some strips fall off?

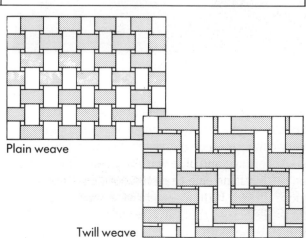

Plain weave

Twill weave

Make a simple loom

You need: a plastic food tray, scissors, string, sellotape, coloured wools, ribbons, plastic strips, etc. for weaving.

What to do

1 Snip each end of the food tray at 1 cm intervals, using a pair of sharp scissors. These grooves will hold the string in position.
2 Wind some string or wool round and round the tray, slotting it each time into the grooves. Tie the string tightly and fix it underneath the tray using sellotape. These are called the **warp threads**.
3 Choose some coloured **weft threads**. You can use wool, ribbons, plastic bag strips — anything! Weave these in and out of the warp threads to create your design.
4 When the weaving is finished, cut the string from underneath the tray. Hang up your work or display it flat.

simple loom weaving

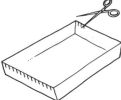
snip plastic tray to make grooves

wind string to make warp threads

weave in the weft threads

display your design

Making a simple loom

To do

How are your clothes woven? From your work with paper weaving, try and discover how some of the clothes you are wearing are woven. Sort them into
- plain weaves
- twill weave
- others

Use the pictures opposite to help.

Clothes	Plain weave	Twill weave	Others
Shirt	✓		
Jeans		✓	

Plain weave
Used for flat, smooth fabrics such as blouses, shirts, dresses.

Twill weave
This fabric had a **diagonal ridge.** Used for denim jeans, uniforms and gaberdine which is used for skirts and trousers and jackets.

Have a go at weaving – it's a lot of fun! These pages show work by pupils of Hampden Gurney school who took part in a large weaving project.

Looms for weaving on can be made from sticks or pieces of wood wrapped round with string or wool – just use your imagination! All kinds of things can be woven: strips of material, wool, paper, moss… so have a go.

Here a pupil is weaving large strips of paper – it helps to explore different ways to weave patterns before you start.

This picture shows a simple loom where the thread is woven in and out of the warp thread, going down.

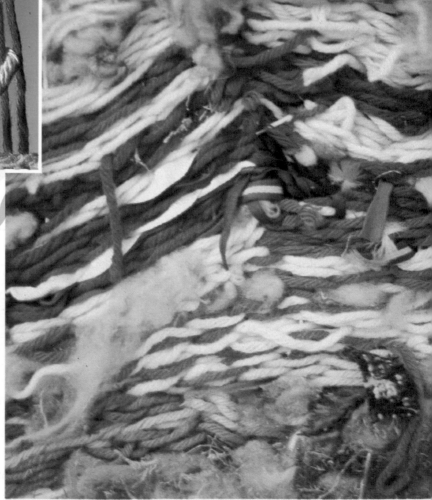

A variety of materials has been woven into this piece of weaving. It makes an interesting wall hanging with rough, smooth, hairy and fluffy textures.

By using different thicknesses of wool you can weave a delicious multi-coloured fabric.

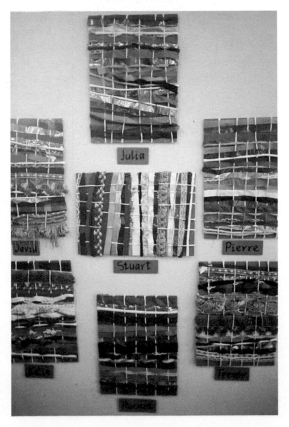

Fabrics can be cut or torn into strips and then woven back into a design of your choice.

Strips of paper and coloured thread used for wrapping presents have been woven into these fabrics.

After weaving, knitting is the second most important way of making up fabrics. No one knows where knitting started. Very few old knitted garments survive, because the fabric rots away. Fabrics can be knitted using one, two or many needles. Primitive people knitted fishing nets using one needle.

Most knitwear today is made by knitting machines which use hundreds of needles instead of the 2–4 needles used in hand knitting.

An example of knitting a plastic bag

To do

Knit something for nothing – it's in the bag! Try knitting up some plastic carrier bags. They are cheaper than wool and produce exciting results. Supermarkets and shops often give carrier bags free with purchases. You can find them in brilliant colours – red, green, purple and gold. Thicker quality bags produce the best results. Try black bin liners, too.

You need: a collection of coloured bags, size 6-7 mm needles, sharp scissors.

You can make a sweatband, headband or wrist band. When you have more practice, move on to waistcoats, tops, bow ties and even skirts – all for free! Sew up your work using a large needle and your plastic 'thread'.

What to do

1 Snip the top edge off the bag with the scissors. Use the scissor blade to cut strips about 1-1½ cm wide working round and round the bag. Try not to break the strip.

2 Cut the length of plastic that you need then you can keep your knitting in the uncut bag!

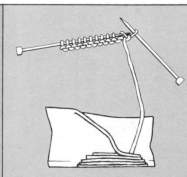

3 Now, using large needles, have a go at knitting a bag. Ask for help if necessary. To start with cast on about 10 stitches. Knit several rows in plain knitting.

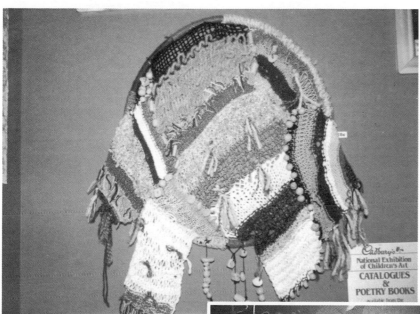

A knitted hoop

Knitted hats

This girl is using a knitting machine

Further work

1   Make a list of as many knitted things as you can think of. Compare your list with the rest of the class and see who has thought of the most.

2   Find out more about knitting and the different stitches used.

Colouring fabric using dyes

Long before commercial powder dyes were available, people used plants to dye fabrics. They used fruits, especially berries, and also vegetables.

Can you think of a few fruits or vegetables which would dye well? Think about foods which stain your hands when you prepare them or leak colour into the water when boiled.

To do

Try out this activity to find out which fruits and vegetables make good dyes.
You need: fresh, frozen or canned fruit and vegetables, saucepan and lid, wooden spoon, sieve, white paper, jug, teaspoon, two pieces of white fabric per group.

Mali woman dyeing fabric

Trying out fruits and vegetables, to see how well they dye

What to do

1   Copy out this chart and fill in the second column. What colour do you think they will dye the fabric? Try to be precise in how you describe it e.g. pale pink.

Fruit or vegetable	What colour do you think it will dye the fabric?	Results	
		a) Colour of fabric	b) Colour using cream of tartar
Beetroot Spinach Onion Blackberry Red cabbage Cherry Carrot			

54

2. Work with a partner. Cut up about 100 g of one of the fruits or vegetables. Do not peel.
3. Put the pieces in a saucepan with 750 ml water.
4. Bring to the boil and then simmer with the lid on for about 10 minutes.
5. Sieve out the pieces and keep the coloured water.
6. Place one piece of plain white cotton or calico (about 20 cm^2) into the saucepan and soak for at least 15 minutes.
7. Mix together 125 ml water and 1 teaspoon of cream of tartar. Soak a second piece of fabric (marked with a pin) in this solution for 5-10 minutes. Then squeeze out the water from the fabric and place in dye as well.

8. After about 15 minutes remove each piece of fabric onto white paper to dry.
9. Fill in the chart with the details from other groups.

Questions

1. Which fruit or vegetable gave (a) the strongest colour, (b) the weakest?
2. Why do you think natural dyes are not often used to colour fabric and clothes today?
3. The mixture of water and cream of tartar used in the activity above is called a **mordant**. Use other books to find out and explain what a mordant is.

Tie and dye

You can knot, twist, gather and tightly bind fabric with string before **dyeing** to get **patterns**. The tighter the string is tied the less the dye will be absorbed – this will give the pattern. It is also important to use quite a bit of string for a good effect.

Two ways of tying the fabric: (a) in 'bunches', (b) folding it backwards and forwards like a fan

To do

Try tie and dye for yourself.
You need: fabric, scissors, string, dye, bucket, rubber gloves, small bits of card.
1. First tie up your fabric using plenty of string.
2. Mix the dye according to the instructions. Be careful not to get any on your hands or clothes.
3. Leave a long piece of string so that you can dip the fabric in the dye and pull it out easily. Add a name tag to this if required.
4. Wet the tied fabric in a bowl of water.
5. Soak in the dye until it has a good colour (about 15-20 minutes). Rinse in cold water to remove excess dye.
6. Dry before removing the string and then iron out creases.

A piece of fabric which has been tied and dyed

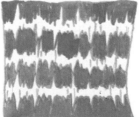

The results of dyeing, using two ways of tying

Question

1. What are the most popular colours? Conduct a survey to find out what colours people in your class are wearing. Work out which colour is the most popular. Is there a reason for its popularity?

If you look very closely at patterns, you will see that most are made up of a few very **simple shapes**. These shapes can be **repeated** and moved around to make up a **complicated design**. Before you go ahead and start printing patterns onto fabric, try these activities to help you understand how to make patterns of your own from simple shapes. This pattern is made from the following shapes.

shapes

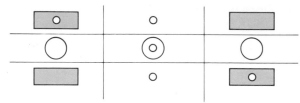

pattern 1

Questions

1 How many times has each shape been used? Copy the tally chart opposite and fill in the results.

shape	tally of how many times used	number
▭	1111	4
◯		
○		

2 Design your own pattern from the shapes below.

shapes

Copy this grid and fill in your pattern.

pattern 2

3 Design your own pattern using shapes of your own choice. What shapes did you use? Draw them out on a chart.

shapes I used were

Copy the grid and fill in your pattern.

my pattern

4 The design for the pattern opposite is quite complicated, yet it is still made up of simple shapes. Copy the chart below and fill in your results.

Shapes used	How many times are they used?

pattern

Wooden block printing

Shapes can be printed onto fabric using **wooden blocks** which have been **carved** into a pattern. The picture shows a lady in India printing a pattern onto fabric, having first dipped the block into printing ink. Gradually she builds up a pattern or design. In the spaces, she may well use another block to print a pattern in a different design.

Using a block for printing

Roller printing

A roller which is used for printing

For **large scale** fabric printing, designs are cut into **copper rollers**. The roller is brushed with printing paste and **rolled over** the fabric, so printing on the design.

A woman and her child, wearing printed fabric

This mother and child are wearing garments printed in many different colours. Each colour is printed separately. It takes a long time to produce the final design and this could make the fabric expensive.

Fabrics used as clothes, furniture and curtains would be very boring if there were no patterns on them. Patterns are printed on to add colour and variety.

To do

Have a go at printing. You can print onto paper, fabrics or clothes, such as T-shirts or shorts, using **fabric paint** or **printing ink**.

Before you start, points to remember
- If you are using new fabric, wash and dry it first.
- Cover the table or work surface with old newspaper.
- Put layers of paper or card between the front and back of a shirt.
- Protect your own clothes with an apron or old shirt.
- Keep your hands clean as you work to prevent smudges.
- Dry and follow the manufacturer's instructions for setting your print on to the fabric. You may need a hot iron for this.

Fabric pens

You can buy special felt tip pens or crayons which you can use to draw straight onto the fabric. **First** wash and dry the fabric. Sketch your idea on paper and then **practise** on a scrap of fabric to get the feel of the pens.

Put some paper **underneath** the fabric or **between** the front and the back of the garment. Stretch out the fabric and **secure** with clips. Draw your design **carefully**, make sure that you do not smudge it, and then follow the manufacturer's instructions to **set** it on the fabric.

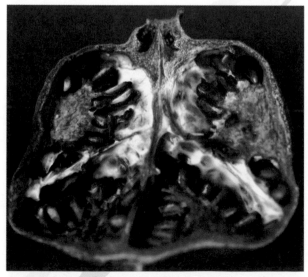

A cross-section of pomegranate

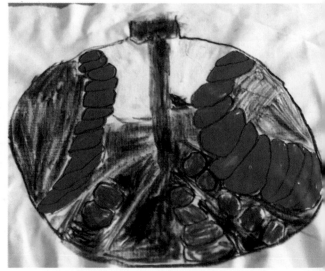

The cross-section of a pomegranate has been copied onto white fabric, using fabric pens by Bruno Duarte, age 13

Transfer crayons and paints

Transfer crayons and paints can be used to draw a design onto paper. This design is then **transferred** onto clean fabric using a hot iron, following manufacturer's instructions. To re-use the same design, you just recolour and print again. As each design comes out **back to front**, you must **remember** to write letters back to front too. You can always use fabric pens to write on the words later, though. The designs for 'Lollipops' and 'Fish' have both been transferred from paper artwork, using transfer crayons, onto fabric.

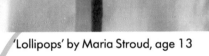

'Lollipops' by Maria Stroud, age 13

'Fish' by Jason Gilbert, age 14

'Dragonfly Drape' is a press print designed by Ronald Day, age 10

'Fruit Cocktail' is a printed fabric designed by Lindsey Blackley, age 15

Potato printing

To do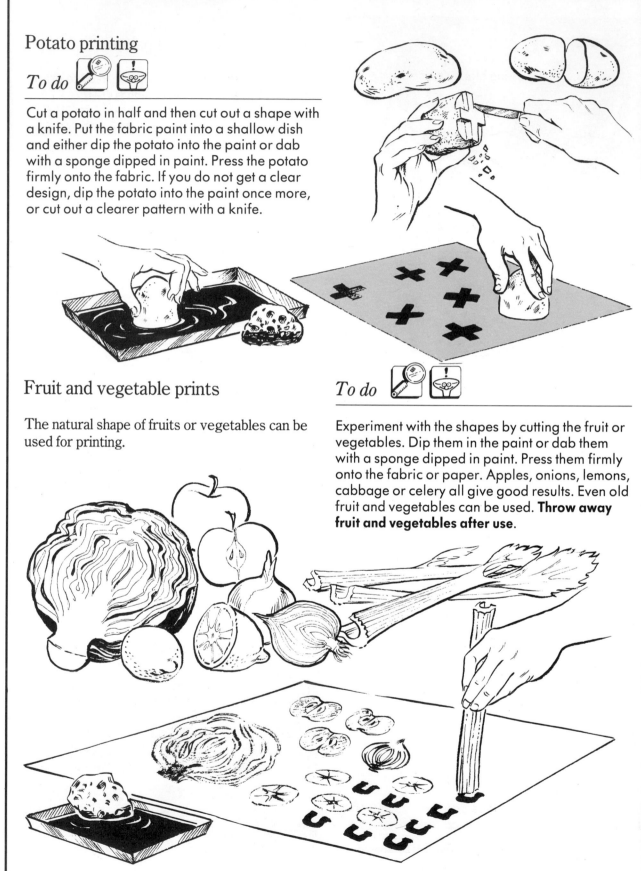

Cut a potato in half and then cut out a shape with a knife. Put the fabric paint into a shallow dish and either dip the potato into the paint or dab with a sponge dipped in paint. Press the potato firmly onto the fabric. If you do not get a clear design, dip the potato into the paint once more, or cut out a clearer pattern with a knife.

Fruit and vegetable prints

The natural shape of fruits or vegetables can be used for printing.

To do

Experiment with the shapes by cutting the fruit or vegetables. Dip them in the paint or dab them with a sponge dipped in paint. Press them firmly onto the fabric or paper. Apples, onions, lemons, cabbage or celery all give good results. Even old fruit and vegetables can be used. **Throw away fruit and vegetables after use.**

String prints

You can make a 'printing block' from string and card.

To do

Glue a design onto an old cereal packet or other card using medium-thick parcel string and PVA glue. Let the glue dry and then dab the string with a small piece of sponge dipped in fabric paint or ink. Press it firmly onto the fabric.

Using stencils

Stencils are pieces of card with holes cut into them.

To do

Draw your pattern onto card. Delicate designs are difficult. Cut out the areas which you want to print. Put the stencil onto the fabric. Use a big stiff brush to dab paint onto the fabric.
If you want a 'splatter' effect, then use an old nailbrush.

Questions

1 Which fruits or vegetables gave the best printed results?
2 Out of the four methods on these pages, which method might be used by textile designers to print fabrics? Give your reasons.

Stencilling onto fabric

Patchwork quilts

For hundreds of years, men, women and children have all sewn pieces of fabric together to make **patchwork**. Often old or left-over bits of material were used and the patchwork was made into **quilts**, **cushions** and **clothing**.

People who study the history of textiles think quilts are an important link. Pieces of material, some as much as 300 years old from frocks and curtains, have been found in quilts.

During the Crimean War some British soldiers made patchwork blankets using scraps of uniform cloth. Here, Private Thomas Walker is working on triangular pieces of patchwork as he recovers from his injuries.

Many shapes can be joined together to make a patchwork. Some of these shapes may be **polygons** - straight sided shapes.

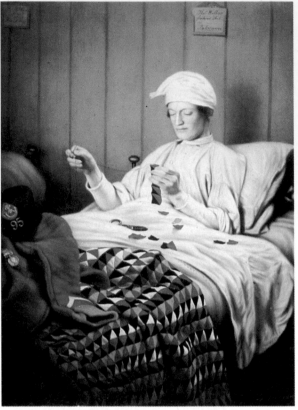

Private Thomas Walker sewing patchwork

Polygons

(1) (2) (3) (4)

(5) (6) (7) (8)

To do

Match up the shapes shown above, with their correct names. Write the number, then the name, e.g.

● (1) is a square

Names
diamond   trapezium   triangle
hexagon   square   parallelogram
rectangle   octagon

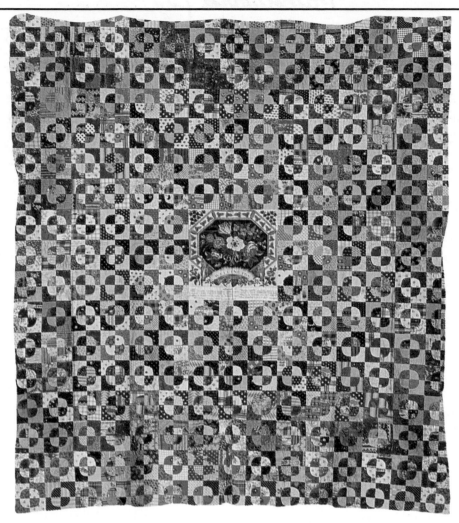

A patchwork quilt made in 1829

This picture shows part of a patchwork quilt made in 1829. The octagonal piece in the centre has the word 'Wellington' printed on it. These centres were printed to remind people of the Duke of Wellington's victory at the Battle of Vittoria in 1813. Below the centre piece are the names 'John and Elizabeth Chapman 1829'. They were probably the owners of the quilt. There are also these words:

> 'O luck husband blest of heaven
> To thee the privilege is given
> A much loved wife at home to keep,
> Caress, touch, talk to - even sleep
> Thrice happy mortal envied lot
> What a rare treasure thou hast (got)
> Who to a woman can lay claim
> Whose temper's every day the same'

Questions

1. What shapes have been used to make this quilt?
2. How does this piece of verse remind the husband of his wife's good qualities?
3. Invent a piece of verse about yourself. You could print it out on a computer. Perhaps you could use it for a T-shirt design.

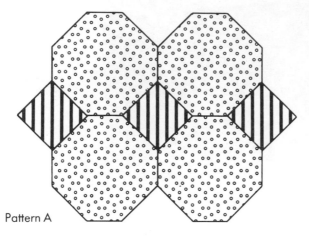

Pattern A

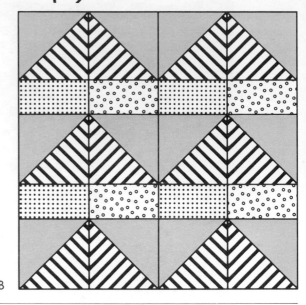

Pattern B

To do

1. Two different shapes have been used for each of these patchwork patterns. Name the shapes used in pattern A and pattern B.
2. Measure **exactly** one of the polygons on page 62. Copy it onto a sheet of centimetre-squared paper measuring about 20 cm by 20 cm. Repeat this shape, and add others if necessary as part of a design for your own piece of patchwork. Colour in your design.

Traditional patchwork patterns

These two patterns, 'Wedding Rings' and 'Goose Tracks', have been used for many years in patchwork quilt designs.

They are both **symmetrical**. That is, if you drew a line down the middle of each pattern, one half would be a **mirror image** of the other.

'Wedding Rings'

'Goose Tracks'

Questions

1. What shapes are used in each of these traditional patterns?
2. Why do you think the names were chosen?

This modern quilt, made from black and white pieces, was designed by Pat Novy. It is called 'A walk in the garden'

To do

1 Draw *four* of the different shapes which are used in the patchwork. Try and name each one. Invent a name for those which you do not know.

2 Why do you think the quilt is called 'A walk in the garden'?

3 On squared paper design a patchwork quilt, using any shape that you choose. It may be symmetrical or non-symmetrical like the one above. Give your design a name and colour it.

4 You may like to make up a real piece of patchwork using scraps of fabric. These pieces can be sewn together by hand or machine. Use other books to help you.

What is a design brief?

A **design brief** is a problem or task that you have to solve and work through. Here is a design brief from one school.

Design a glove puppet that you will use for a school puppet show at Hallowe'en. You can use 25 cm squares of felt and scrap pieces of material.

Louise Davies with pupils

Pupil with a puppet

So – how do you start? **First**, read the brief
carefully. **Then**, sort out your order of work… .

1   Think about **ideas** for your design.

2   Draw your design on paper. Add details like
hair and teeth.

3   Draw a pattern around your hand on squared
paper. Allow space for your hand to move.

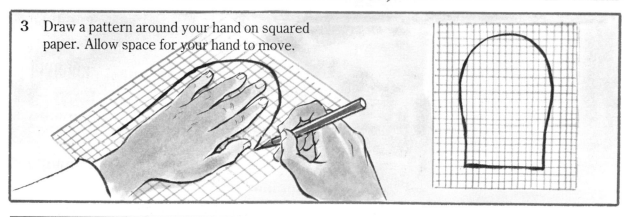

4   Choose the colour of your felt, thread and
extra scraps.

5   Pin your pattern onto felt and cut out two
pieces – front and back. Don't forget pieces
for ears, nose and hat.

6   Pin into place – you can change pieces if you
need to.

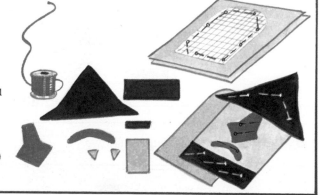

7 Sew your puppet together and try it out.

8 Fill in your evaluation sheet.

Name *Mark out of 10 for*	Me	My teacher
my ideas for the design		
my sketches		
cutting the pattern		
cutting the fabric		
sewing up the puppet		
the finished puppet		
working by myself		
how well I worked		
helping other people		
clearing up afterwards		
listening		
organizing myself and my work		
The things I did well:		
The ways I could have done better:		
The part I enjoyed most:		
Did my puppet turn out as well as I wanted?		yes/no
Why?		

9 Now prepare your puppet show.

Carnival!

Design for carnival

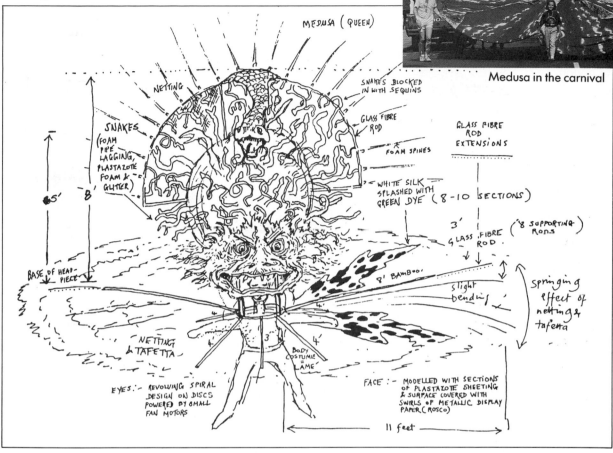

Medusa in the carnival

The design for Medusa, the Carnival Queen

Every year, hundreds of people are involved in the creation of themes and inventions for the Notting Hill Carnival. Several months before the carnival, the **Mas Makers** start work. (These are the people who organize the parade of glittering costume bands.) First they decide upon a **theme** for their band. Next they work out a **design brief** which includes costumes for the masqueraders, the spectacular designs for the 'king' and 'queen' and the decoration for the float which carries the band of musicians.

In October 1987, Martha Fevrier and Billy Nicholas got together and decided that the **theme** for their band, Flamingo, in 1988 would be **Myths and Legends**. Using library books to help, Billy painted the costumes. Then he drew up plans for them to be made. These included the Carnival Queen, Medusa the Gorgon, with her head of hissing snakes. Billy's drawing shows the materials he used for the Medusa costume.

When Billy creates his costume three main factors affect its design.

1 Gusts of **wind** can blow over a poorly designed costume. So Billy measures it to make sure the costume will not be too wide or too tall. Fabrics must be chosen to let the wind through, otherwise they act like a sail and carry the wearer along!
2 The costume must not be too **heavy**. So lightweight materials such as bamboo, cane and foam are used for head and body shapes and thin fabrics for costumes.
3 The band only has a little money. So Martha shops for fabrics in local markets, and costumes are made using cheap materials. The snakes on Medusa's head are made from pipe lagging and covered in glittery shapes.

Volunteers, including school children, work on the costumes, cutting, sewing and sticking them together. On the Sunday of Carnival, nearly 80 children take part in the Flamingo band as it dances through the streets of Notting Hill in London.

Medusa, the Flamingo Queen, leading the procession

Martha and Billy, the designers of the Flamingo band

Billy Nicholas with his designs and finished 'snakes'

Billy constructing the head out of cane

Now for the eyes

The head with snakes is ready

The huge skirt is laid out

The Flamingo band in the carnival

Question

Think of your own theme for carnival. Design and label a costume for your queen and king.

Dirty clothes

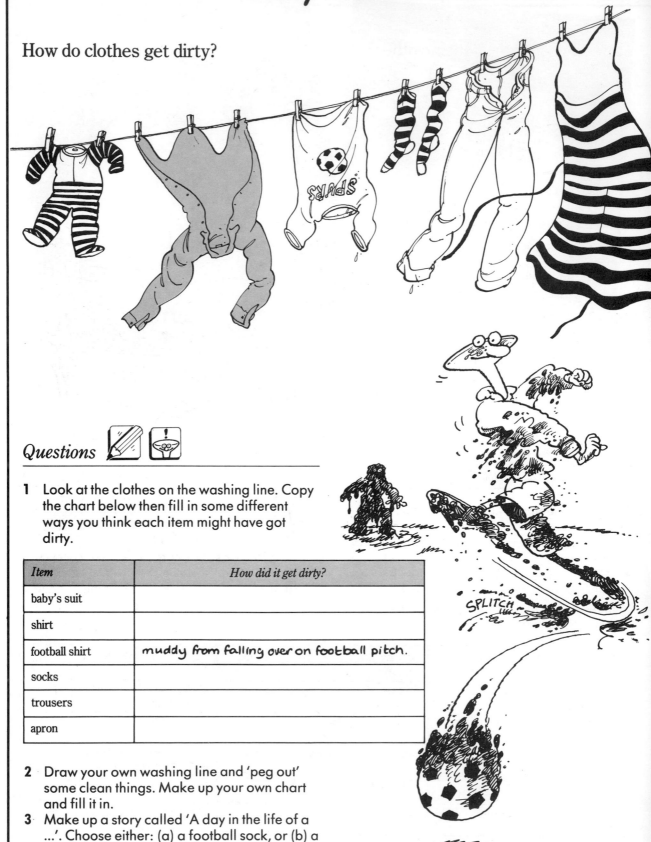

How do clothes get dirty?

Questions

1 Look at the clothes on the washing line. Copy the chart below then fill in some different ways you think each item might have got dirty.

Item	How did it get dirty?
baby's suit	
shirt	
football shirt	muddy from falling over on football pitch.
socks	
trousers	
apron	

2 Draw your own washing line and 'peg out' some clean things. Make up your own chart and fill it in.

3 Make up a story called 'A day in the life of a ...'. Choose either: (a) a football sock, or (b) a cookery apron. In your story describe how the item got really dirty and then clean again.

How do people wash their clothes?

To do

Carry out a **survey** to find out how people wash their clothes. Ask the following questions.
- Do you usually wash clothes by machine or by hand?
- What powder or liquids do you use?
- Why do you choose these products?

Interview up to ten different people. Copy and fill in a chart like the one below.

When all the class has completed their surveys, collect together the information. Find out whether most people wash by machine or hand, and which are the most popular washing products.

Interview	Machine or hand wash	What powder or liquid do they use?	What is the reason?
Mum	Machine	Persil Powder and Comfort or Lenor Liquid	Gets clothes clean and fresh
Dad	Machine	Ariel Powder	Nice smell
Gran	Hand	Dreft and Bio-tex powder	Likes the brand and gets clothes clean
Aunt H.	Machine	Persil and Comfort	Less static electricity in clothes
Friend at school. Arfan	Machine	Bold 3	Likes the smell and gets clothes clean

The results of a survey about how people wash their clothes

Dirty clothes are washed in water, but is water on its own enough, or does it need help?

To do

Find out if water is good at wetting fabrics. Work in small groups.

Each group needs: a pipette, a bowl, a piece of paper or closely woven fabric, washing up liquid, detergent washing powder.

What to do

1 Fill the pipette with cold water from the bowl.
2 Put the paper or fabric on the work surface and squeeze on three drops of water. Carefully draw a side view of the drops.
3 Leave 'drop 1' as the **control** – that is, you do nothing to it.
   Squeeze a drop of washing up liquid from the bottle or using the pipette onto 'drop 2'.
   Sprinkle a little detergent washing powder onto 'drop 3'. Now draw the results.
   Look at the underneath of your paper/fabric and see how wet each drop made it.
   Copy the chart below and fill in your results.

drop 1   drop 2   drop 3

drop 1

Surface tension

Drop	What was added to the drop?	What happened?	How wet was the paper/fabric?
Drop 1	nothing		
Drop 2	washing up liquid		
Drop 3	detergent washing powder		

Why is it difficult for water to wet things?

The water on the paper or fabric made a rounded droplet. This is because the **molecules** of water inside the droplet are **strongly attracted** to each other. They form a **force barrier**, called **surface tension**, on the outside of the droplet. This surface tension stops the water from **wetting** things easily.

If **detergent**, like washing up liquid or powder, is added, the surface tension is **broken**. The droplet breaks up and wets the paper or fabric.

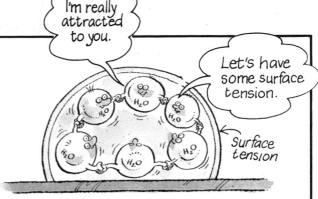

surface tension on a droplet of water.

detergent breaks down the surface tension.

How do detergents work?

Three things are needed to remove dirt from fabric.
- water
- detergent
- movement.

Water needs **detergent** to help **wet** fabric.

Detergent can get between the fabric and the dirt and **loosen** the dirt.

Movement such as **scrubbing** or **swirling** in a washing machine then **shakes the dirt off**.

Detergent molecules **surround** the dirt, **remove** it and leave behind clean clothes!

Questions

1 What does 'the surface tension of a droplet of water' mean?
2 What does detergent do to surface tension?
3 What *three* things are needed to remove dirt from fabrics?
4 How can detergents help get things clean?
5 How does movement help get rid of dirt?

Soap was not used for cleaning until the 1st century AD. Before that time people washed themselves and their clothes with a clay-like substance that loosens oil and dirt.

The first soap was made by boiling pieces of fat in an iron pot then adding wood ash, called **lye**. This produced a soft, yellowy soap. A hard soap could be made by boiling it longer and adding salt.

In Britain, soap was a luxury and was taxed by the government until 1853. Clothes were not washed very often. One Scottish clergyman, who couldn't stand the smell in his church any longer asked that people 'improve upon the practice of cleansing their church clothes once a year at Easter.'

In Victorian times, clothes were washed in tubs of water and pounded with a **dolly** – a three-legged stool – to loosen the dirt. Commercial laundries opened in the 1860s. By the 1950s washing machines were familiar in many homes. Soap was replaced by new, **low lather detergent powders**.

Home laundry in the 19th century

A **detergent** is 'a substance which helps remove dirt'. Detergents were discovered by two German chemists. During the First World War there was a shortage of the animal fat needed to make soap. The chemists invented a detergent, a kind of artificial soap which was made from **complex chemicals** instead of **fat**. By the 1950s these new **soapless detergents** were widely used. In the 1960s **enzymes** were added to some powders to help **remove stains**. Recently washing powders which work at **low temperatures** have been introduced.

What's in a washing powder?

Many ingredients make up modern automatic washing powders.
Here are some.

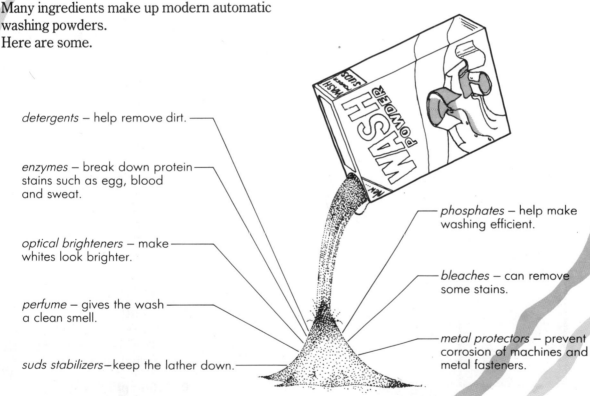

detergents – help remove dirt.

enzymes – break down protein stains such as egg, blood and sweat.

optical brighteners – make whites look brighter.

perfume – gives the wash a clean smell.

suds stabilizers – keep the lather down.

phosphates – help make washing efficient.

bleaches – can remove some stains.

metal protectors – prevent corrosion of machines and metal fasteners.

Questions

1 How has the washing of clothes changed over the years?
2 What does 'detergent' mean?
3 In modern washing powders, why are:
   (a) metal protectors,
   (b) suds stabilizers,
   (c) optical brighteners added?
4 Use a dictionary or other books to find out what these words mean: (a) lather
   (b) corrosion (c) enzymes (d) bleaches

Collect together as many empty packets of washing powder as possible, to give you ideas.

First – invent a name

Names should be short and punchy. Washing product names often remind us of clean things. What do these names remind you of?

This is what some pupils thought:

Annabel   'Daz is like the word "dazzling".'
Ken   'Fairy reminds me of soft and gentle.'

Two logos used on washing powders

Second – design a logo for your washing powder

A logo is the drawing design for your name. Draw a square or rectangle, then fill in your idea and colour your design.

Third – invent a slogan

A **slogan** is a catchy phrase about your washing powder. Here are some used on real packets.

Bold – Deep down clean, soft, fresh
Surf – So clean you can smell it's clean

Finally work out an advert

Your idea could be:
- a poster or page in a **magazine**,
- a radio advert using a **jingle** with music,
- a **TV advert**.

What's in a name?

The history of the name 'Lux'

Lux soap flakes were first called 'Sunlight Flakes', but this was not a popular name, so in 1899 the owner changed the name to **Lux**. *Lux* in Latin means 'light', so it was a suitable, short name to use, which also made people think of 'luxury'. Eighty years later, the product is still being sold.

(Dictionary of Trade Names, A. Room)

This advert for Lux was used in 1905

Questions

1 What claims does the advert make about Lux? Do any of these claims surprise you?
2 Why do you think the slogan says 'Why don't they use Lux!!'?
3 Do you think this is a good advert? Give your reasons.

To do

Make a collection of adverts for washing products, and empty packets of washing powder. As a class, discuss which adverts you like best and why, and which adverts you think are not very effective (the ones which don't catch your eye, or look attractive).

Look closely at the washing powder packets. Which ones do you think are well designed? Think of as many reasons as possible for this 'good design'.

Follow the flow chart and design your own washing powder packet.

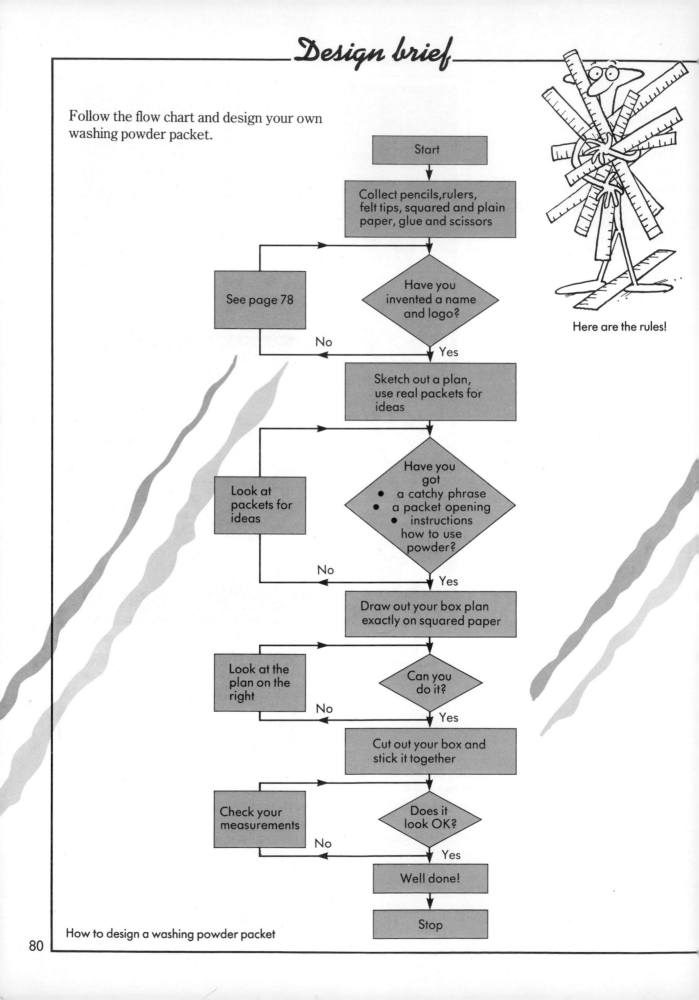

Start

Collect pencils, rulers, felt tips, squared and plain paper, glue and scissors

See page 78

Have you invented a name and logo?

No → Yes

Sketch out a plan, use real packets for ideas

Look at packets for ideas

Have you got
- a catchy phrase
- a packet opening
- instructions how to use powder?

No → Yes

Draw out your box plan exactly on squared paper

Look at the plan on the right

Can you do it?

No → Yes

Cut out your box and stick it together

Check your measurements

Does it look OK?

No → Yes

Well done!

Stop

Here are the rules!

How to design a washing powder packet

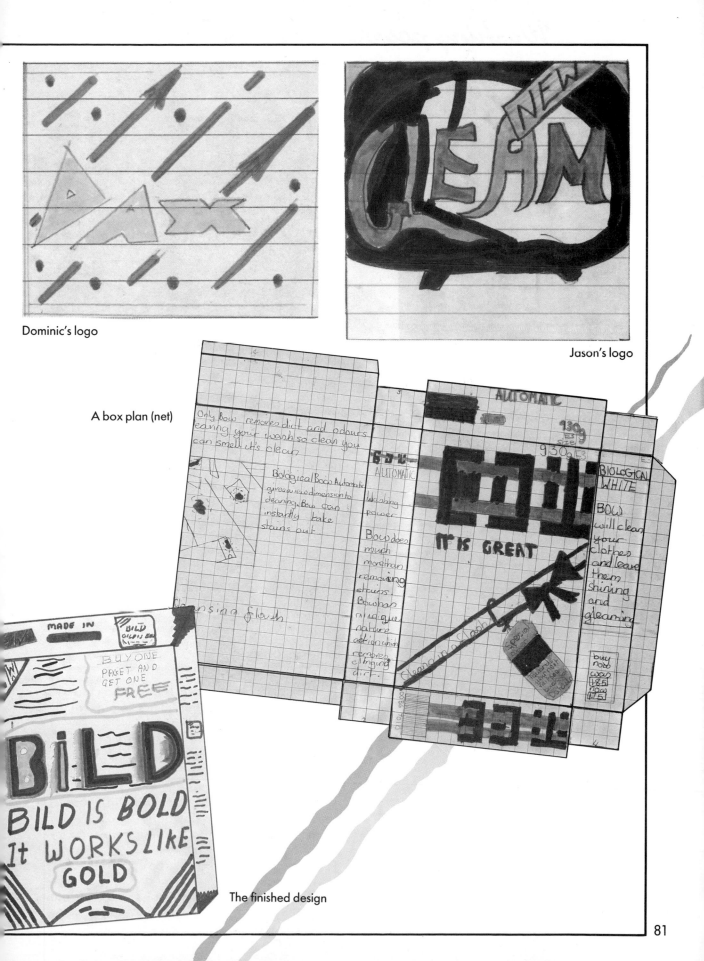

Dominic's logo

Jason's logo

A box plan (net)

Only Bow removes dirt and odours leaving your wash so clean you can smell it's clean

Biological Bow Automatic gives a new dimension to cleaning. Bow can instantly take stains out.

Cleansing flash

 GO-U-AUTOMATIC washing power

Bow does much more than removing stains. Bow has unique nature action which removes clinging dirt.

AUTOMATIC

930g SIZE

930g E3

E3

COW IT IS GREAT

Cleaning in a flash

SPECIAL

BIOLOGICAL WHITE

BOW will clean your clothes and leave them shining and gleaming

buy now was £1.85 now £1.5

MADE IN

BILD GILDIS BOW

BUY ONE PACKET AND GET ONE FREE

BiLD
BILD IS BOLD
It WORKS LIKE
GOLD

The finished design

ARIEL AUTOMATIC

E3 SIZE. AUTOMATIC WASHING POWDER WITH BIOLOGICAL ACTION AND BLEACHING AND BRIGHTENING AGENTS

USE THE RIGHT AMOUNT OF POWDER

MAINWASH ONLY IN AUTOMATIC MACHINES

Use 2 cups

Light soiling or small loads may need less powder — especially in soft water. Heavy soiling may need up to 4 cups

FOR TOUGH WASHING PROBLEMS USE THE PRE-WASH

For pre-wash use 1½ cups followed by 1½ cups in the mainwash

HANDWASHING AND SOAKING

SOAKING GARMENTS WILL GIVE YOU EVEN BETTER RESULTS

1. Check the articles are suitable for soaking Clothes with washing codes 95°, 60° and 50° are normally suitable.

2. Use ½ a cup in a bowl or bucket.

3. Dissolve powder before immersing clothes in solution.

4. After soaking, rinse thoroughly before drying.

NEVER
soak non-colourfast fabrics, silk, wool, leather garments with metal fasteners or flame resistant finishes.

DO NOT
use an enamel bath for soaking.

HAND CARE
After any washing job other than in your machine rinse your hands and dry them thoroughly. People with sensitive or damaged skin should pay particular attention to the usage instructions and avoid prolonged contact with the washing solution.

€ 1.05 kg E3 SIZE

ARIEL AUTOMATIC

108P

IMPROVED CLEANING

NEW

EVEN AT LOWER TEMPERATURES

House Plants

SEND FOR A FREE House Plants Book
SEE BACK OF PACK

How to use washing powders

Questions

Look at the Ariel packet label and picture.

1 How much does this E3 packet: (a) weigh, (b) cost?
2 What does this washing powder contain? Why do you think it is called 'Automatic'?
3 How much powder is used in an automatic washing machine? When might you need to add: (a) more powder, (b) less powder?
4 What do you think is a 'tough washing problem'?
5 How may this powder be used for handwashing?
6 What things should not be soaked? Explain why.

Fabric conditioners

Washing can make cottons and knitwear harsh to touch. Synthetic, chemically made fibres, such as nylon, can produce **static electricity** which makes clothes **cling**.

What do fabric conditioners do?

- They soften fabrics.
- They reduce static electricity.
- They help make ironing easier.

To do

Find out more about static electricity.

You need: a balloon, someone wearing a blazer or jumper, tiny pieces of scrap paper or pieces from hole punching.

What to do
1 Blow up and tie the balloon.
2 Rub the balloon up and down the sleeve of the blazer or jumper for about 30 seconds.
3 Hold the balloon over the pieces of paper.

What happens?
The balloon should pick up the pieces of paper.

Why?
Static electricity is produced by **friction**. Rubbing the balloon up and down the sleeve **charges** it with static electricity. This static electricity makes the pieces of paper cling to the balloon.

How can static electricity affect clothes?
Synthetic fibres can produce static electricity, which makes the clothes **cling** and sometimes **crackle** and **sparkle**. Fabric conditioners can reduce the effect of static electricity.

Questions

Look at the photographs below.
1 How has the fabric conditioner changed the shape of the fibres in the photographs?
2 Explain, in your own words, what you think a fabric conditioner does.

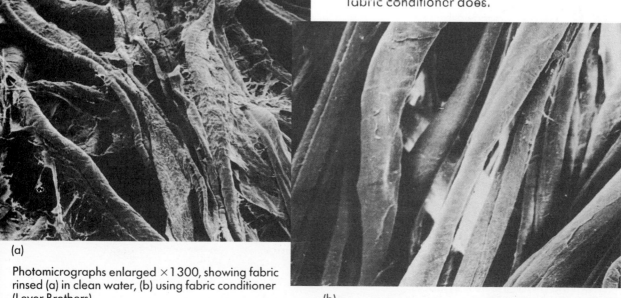

(a)

Photomicrographs enlarged ×1300, showing fabric rinsed (a) in clean water, (b) using fabric conditioner (Lever Brothers)

(b)

With all the improvements in fabrics, washing machines and detergents, washing has become a complicated business.

In 1987 the care labels on clothes and household fabrics had new **wash tub symbols**. The **number** inside the wash tub is the **temperature** of the water to be used for washing.

Old	New	
1 95	95	
2 60	60	Cotton wash cycle at hot and medium temperatures
3 60	60	
4 50	50	Man-made, easy care cotton and blends of fibres which need medium washing condition
6 40	40	
7 40	40	Wool wash cycle with low temperature, gentle wash
Handwash	Handwash	Handwash (do not machine wash)
Do not wash	Do not wash	Do not wash

New and old washing symbols

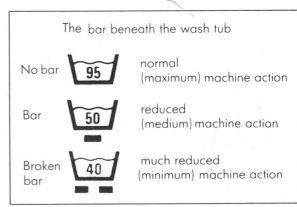

The bar beneath the wash tub

No bar	95	normal (maximum) machine action
Bar	50	reduced (medium) machine action
Broken bar	40	much reduced (minimum) machine action

New washing symbols sometimes have bars

Questions

1 Spot *three* changes which have been made from the old to the new symbols.
2 What do the bars under the wash tub mean?

Other symbols used on care labels

Now I see – you need care labels to help care for your clothes.

 Chlorine bleach may be used

 Do not use chlorine bleach

 Warm iron
an iron with one dot (·) means cool
an iron with three dots (···) means hot

 Do not iron

Bleaching and ironing symbols

Tumbling and dry cleaning symbols

May be tumble dried

Do not tumble dry

May be dry cleaned

Do not dry clean

To do

Look at the three care labels opposite. Copy the chart and fill in the details. Some have already been completed.

Label	Fabric	Fabric symbol	Washing symbols	Washing instructions
1	Shetland wool			gentle wash on 40° wool cycle, warm iron but no tumbling dry
2	cotton			
3	polyester metallized			

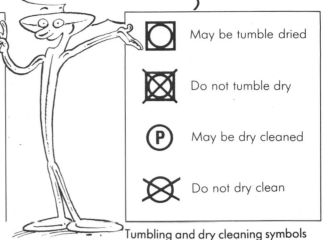

Care labels

Quick quiz

Cover up the symbols on the opposite page and above and test your memory on these 10 symbols for care labels.
1 'handwash'
2 'do not wash'
3 'wool washing'
4 'dry clean'
5 'do not tumble dry'
6 'chlorine bleach can be used'
7 'do not iron'
8 'do not dry clean'
9 'cool iron'
10 temperature for the hottest wash

Further work

Design your own care label for a white cotton shirt. Draw the symbols and describe how to wash and iron the shirt.

Crumpled clothes need to be pressed flat with an **iron**. Years ago, ironing was a tiring and messy job. Heavy **flat irons** were heated up on stoves or fires. **Charcoal-heated irons** contained pieces of hot charcoal and needed pumping with bellows to keep them alight. **Electric irons** were sold in the 1890s. At first these irons were very heavy, and had no temperature control. The design improved and they became lighter and easier to use.

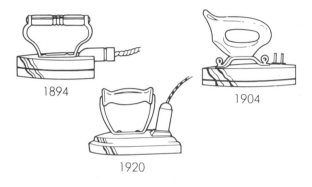

1894   1904

1920

Early types of household electric irons

Charcoal-heated iron

What are steam irons?

Today, of the 4 million irons sold each year, 75% are **steam irons**. Water from the tank of the steam iron is heated and passes as steam through the base of the **sole plate**. Steam irons can be used on all fabrics, but they are particularly good for pressing crumpled things and ironing creases into trousers.

To do 🖊

1 Copy the picture of the steam iron.
2 Match up the labels with the correct numbers.

> *Labels*
> a) *see-through water tank*
> b) *easy-clean sole plate*
> c) *temperature control*
> d) *filling hole*
> e) *spray button*

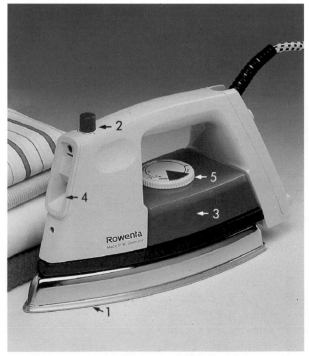

A modern steam iron, the Rowenta 'Tapwater' iron

Questions

1 Why is it useful for a steam iron to have:
   (a) a see-through tank, (b) a temperature control, (c) a spray button?
2 In your own words describe how ironing has changed over the last hundred years.
3 How many of the 4 million irons sold each year are steam irons?

Symbol	Process	Examples of application
	Iron at sole plate temperature of about 120°C (cool iron)	Acrylic, nylon, acetate, triacetate, polyester
	Iron at sole plate temperature of about 160°C (warm iron)	Polyester mixtures wool
	Iron at sole plate temperature of about 210°C (hot iron)	Cotton, linen, viscose or modified viscose
	Do not iron	Detrimental to fabric

Ironing symbols

Ironing symbols

Fabrics need different ironing temperatures to give good results. **Care labels** have **ironing symbols** on them which show heat settings by a series of three dots.

Questions

Use the ironing symbol chart to answer the questions.
1 Draw the iron symbol with dots to give the heat setting for:
   (a) acrylic fabrics, (b) cotton, (c) wool.
2 Which fabrics might have this symbol? Why?

3 What do you think 'detrimental to fabric' means?

To do

Imagine that you had to design a small card for a new brand of iron. Invent a name and design a label. You could use the one on the right. Fill in simple instructions to help someone use the iron safely.

Instructions for Hotto's iron

How was dry cleaning discovered?

In 1825 a maid accidentally spilt some **paraffin** from a lamp onto a dirty tablecloth. Her employer, Monsieur Jean-Baptiste Jolly, a French dyeworks owner, noticed that the paraffin cleaned the cloth and he experimented until he found a **solvent** which cleaned clothes without causing any damage.

Why is dry cleaning necessary?

Some of the clothes we wear have a label which says 'Dry clean only'. Fabrics such as **suede**, **leather** and some **wools** would be ruined if they were washed in water. Other fabrics would **stretch**, **crease** or get **out of shape**. Some fabric dyes would **run** if the clothes were washed in water.

Dry cleaning uses a **solvent**, not water, to **dissolve out grease** and **remove dirt**. Clothes are rotated in the solvent which dissolves fats and greases, and lifts off grit and dirt. This symbol shows that the item should be dry cleaned. The letter in the circle tells the dry cleaner what solvent to use. In this case it is **perchloroethylene**.

Questions

1 Why should some clothes be dry cleaned instead of washed?
2 What is 'dry cleaning'?

3 Write a story with the title 'Ever been taken to the cleaners?'. Use the cartoon to give you ideas.

Washday problems

Labels

To do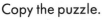

 1

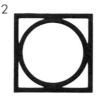 2

 3

 4

 5

 6

 7

8 (P)

9 **E3 SIZE**

10 (heart)

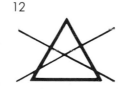 11

 12

 13

 14

1 Can you identify these labels? All except one of these 14 labels have been used somewhere in the book. Write the number of each label and, beside it, the answer e.g. (5) Design Centre London.

2 Find out what *three* of these labels are used for. Copy the chart below and fill in your answers. The missing label has been completed.

Label	*What it stands for*	*How it is used*
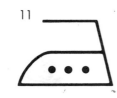	The Design Centre, London.	Products have been selected by the Design Centre – the label says they are well designed.

All washed up?

To do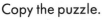

Copy the puzzle.

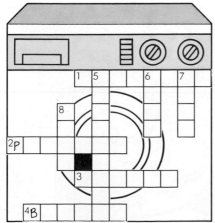

Answer the questions and fill it in.

Across
1 Wash without using a machine (4,4)
2 Added to washing powder to make it smell nice (7)
3 Dirty marks on clothes (6)
4 Added to washing powder to make clothes whiter(6).

Down
5 Special powder used for front loading washing machines (9)
6 A fabric which needs a gentle wash (4)
7 To leave clothes in soapy water (4)
8 A fabric conditioner helps to make clothes _ _ _ _ (4)

A game for 2-6 players

You need: a dice, a counter or coin for each player.

How to play

- Each player throws the dice to start.
- The player moves the counter by the number of squares shown on the dice.
- The winner is the first player to reach the 'Finish'.
- To land on 'Finish', a player must throw the **exact** number needed.

start

throw the dice

Sort out your wardrobe +3

Decide to make your own clothes +3

Jumper shrinks in hot wash −2

Trouser seams split −3

Spend all money on expensive coat −4

Drip-dry shirt – no ironing! +3

Dry cleaning cost £3 −3

Sweat shirt goes saggy −3

Colours run on T-shirt −3

Hand wash only – YUK! −3

Spill tomato ketchup on your trousers −2

Red scarf turns washing pink −3

Borrow a belt and save money +3

Iron too hot – clothing melts −3

Favourite shirt burnt on iron −3

Adapt clothes to suit a new fashion +4

To do

As you play the game make a list of all the plus (+) moves and all the minus (−) moves.
Write down what happens in each case.

Buy clothes in sale +2

Mail order saves time +3

Money off due to mark which you wash off +4

Shirt falls apart — exchange it +1

Adapt clothes from jumble sale +2

Sale goods don't fit −3

Zip broken in trousers −2

Assistant persuades you to overspend −4

Shop around for best bargain +1

Sale goods don't match −2

Use low temperature wash and save money +3

Cut down jeans to make shorts +3

Sell old clothes to your sister +1

Dye your fading T-shirt a new colour +2

finish

91

Why is a T-shirt called a T-shirt?

When a T-shirt is spread flat, it forms the letter T, and so gets its name. T-shirts were invented in the United States in the 1920s as a form of underwear.

Who wore the first cardigan?

At the Charge of Balaclava the Earl of Cardigan led the Light Brigade. He was wearing a knitted woollen waistcoat with sleeves. British soldiers during the 1850s copied the idea of the cardigan to protect themselves from the cold Crimean winter.

And the balaclava?

Well, at the Battle of Balaclava the soldiers kept their heads warm with knitted woollen helmets or caps – and so the name balaclava!

Who invented the mack?

A chemist called Charles Macintosh discovered how to waterproof cloth with India rubber. This cloth was then made into coats which were called after the inventor, but spelt differently – **mackintoshes**.

What about bloomers?

Mrs Amelia Bloomer introduced the bloomer to New York in 1849. She ordered a costume made up of a jacket, skirt and Turkish trousers, to which she gave her name.

Leotards?

A French trapeze artist called Jules Leotard (1842-70) wore a skintight garment for his act. He used to fly over his audience from one trapeze to another. The stretchy body suit, which is worn for gymnastics and dancing, has been called the leotard, after him.

What about the bikini?

Four days after the Americans had exploded the atomic bomb at Bikini Atoll in the Pacific, a French fashion designer called Louis Reard had a fashion show. His model wore a two piece swimming costume, which Mr Reard named 'Bikini', since he thought it was 'the ultimate' – the final straw!'

How did Levis get their name?

Levi Strauss arrived in San Francisco, from Bavaria, during the Gold Rush. He brought with him bales of cloth to make into tents and wagon covers. Seeing the tattered trousers of the miners, Levi had an idea. He made his cloth into hardwearing work trousers and jackets and added rivets to the seams and pockets for strength. Jeans are still made by this method today.

Why are some coats called anoraks?

Greenland Eskimos wore a hooded waterproof jacket for their fishing expeditions in freezing weather. These arctic coats have been copied and sold throughout the world, and are called after their Eskimo name 'Anoraq'.

Quick quiz

1 What costume is named after an atomic bomb explosion?
2 Who gave their name to a pair of knickers?
3 Which trapeze artist gave his name to a stretchy suit?
4 What hat is named after a battle?
5 What is the name of an eskimo's coat?
6 Which Earl liked knitted waistcoats?
7 What famous Bavarian gave his name to a pair of trousers?
8 What garment gets its name from a letter?

Answer the following questions and see how well you have done by adding up your correct answers.

- 15–20 — well done, an excellent score
- 10–15 — nearly there, check your answers and try again.
- below 10 — get reading this book!

1 Which of the following fabrics would make an easy-care apron?
(a) wool (b) cotton (c) PVC

2 Most jumpers are made by
(a) weaving (b) knitting (c) bonding

3 Strong material for trousers should be
(a) woven (b) knitted (c) bonded

4 Which is the odd fibre out?
(a) cotton (b) linen (c) wool (d) jute

5 Why is it different?

6 To soften clothes after washing you can use
(a) washing powder (b) starch
(c) fabric conditioner

7 Which is the odd fibre out?
(a) silk (b) angora (c) camel-hair
(d) rayon (e) alpaca

8 Why is it different?

9 How did the mack get its name?
(a) after a Scottish town (b) after its inventor (c) because of its rubber coating

10 Which fabric is the strongest?
(a) knitted (b) woven (c) bonded

11 The BSI kitemark is a symbol on goods to show
(a) they are cheap (b) they are colourful (c) they are tested for safety

12 Which is the odd garment out?
(a) leotard (b) sari (c) traditional kilt (d) Buddhist monk's clothing

13 Why is it different?

14 Which is the odd fibre out?
(a) lycra (b) tricel (c) nylon
(d) silk (e) terylene

15 Why is it different?

16 Which symbol is used for dry cleaning?

17 How did the bikini get its name?
(a) because it is in 2 pieces (b) after a Japanese town (c) after an atomic explosion

18 How did the leotard get its name?
(a) from a lion skin (b) after a gym club (c) from Mr Leotard

19 What fabric is made from trees?
(a) cotton (b) nylon (c) paper (d) linen

20 Which Earl gave his name to a piece of clothing?
(a) Blazer (b) Cardigan (c) Beret
(d) Knickerbocker

p.17

p.36

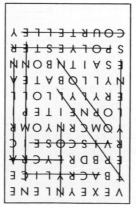

Assess yourself

How well did I work?

After each piece of work, fill in a chart like the one opposite about yourself. Award yourself a mark out of 10 for each section, then answer the three questions underneath.

Sections

a I shared ideas and answers with others.
b I added my own ideas to the lesson.
c I explained things to others.
d I finished all the work.
e I did my best.
f I understood all the work.
g I enjoyed the work.

Questions

1 What was the most interesting thing you learned?
2 What was the most boring part?
3 How could your work improve?

How did you score?

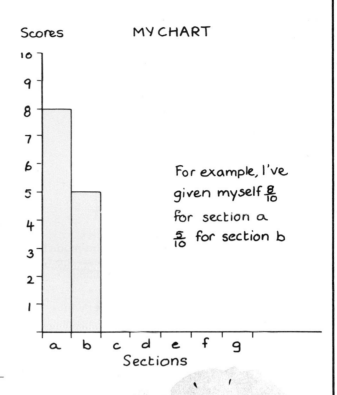

MY CHART

For example, I've given myself $\frac{8}{10}$ for section a $\frac{5}{10}$ for section b

most marks below 5

most marks just over 5

most marks over 7

Answers to p.89

1) pure new wool
2) tumble dry
3) linen trademark
4) BSI safety mark for cookers and gas fires
5) Design Centre
6) cotton
7) hand wash only
8) dry cleanable
9) standard 1.05 kg washing powder
10) BSI kitemark – approved system of control and testing
11) hot iron
12) do not use chlorine bleach
13) reduced washing machine action – 40°C
14) British wool – made from wool in Britain